To the memory of Liberty Rothschild
who drew the cyclamen on the cover

THE ANXIOUS GARDENER

Rozsika Parker
with Dylan Singh

Drawings by Jean Sturgis

FRANCES LINCOLN LIMITED
PUBLISHERS

Frances Lincoln Limited
4 Torriano Mews
Torriano Avenue
London NW5 2RZ
www.franceslincoln.com

British Library Cataloguing in Publication data
A catalogue record for this book is available from the British Library.

ISBN 10: 0-7112-2663-6
ISBN 13: 978-0-7112-2663-0

Printed and bound in Singapore
by Craft Print International Ltd.

2 4 6 8 9 7 5 3 1

CONTENTS

'To be without anxiety was to be without love.'
John McGahern, *That They May Face the Rising Sun*

'Gardening is one of those happy arts in which
there is always some not quite certain change, to
look forward to and to be anxious about.'
Jane Loudon, *The Ladies Country Companion:
How to Enjoy Country Life Rationally*

'Children are a plant substitute and we
haven't the wit to see it until too late.'
Jill Tweedie, *Guardian*

'Anxiety was seen to be the main motivation that
promotes development, although excessive anxiety
can have the opposite effect, when it is
overwhelming and unmanageable.'
Ricky Emanuel, *Anxiety*

AUTUMN

Scarlet geraniums sporting stalks like chicken legs and paltry flowers

The anxious gardener
broods on window boxes

September is the month when the Anxious Gardener begins to worry about winter coats and winter window boxes. Status symbols, they signify conditions inside the house and inside the body. The AG considers her options. Should she go formal with a stark arrangement of Belgravia blue topiary for the house, and single-breasted black wool for the body? Perhaps she should opt for tumbling colour with touches of the country for the boxes, and faux-fur for the coat? Or maybe the answer is to go for soft suede and an understated rose or two. On the other hand, tweed is fashionable and a massed rank of bulbs peeping through something spring-like suggests a horticultural mind at work indoors. Hunting out her mobile she dispatches a cry for help.

'It depends where your priorities lie,' replies the Gardening Mentor. 'Decide whether your boxes are to be inward or outward looking. If viewed from within you need to place the larger specimens in the front of the box, if viewed primarily from the street, then put the bigger plants at the back.'

'I want to please everyone,' cries the AG. 'I want to be loved for my mind and my body.'

'That counts out ornamental cabbages,' replies the GM. 'They display nothing but stalks to the street, but they look a treat from indoors, particularly when planted with heathers, although you could argue that heathers and cabbages are too last year. I've noticed this year a couple of sills housing phormiums, despite the fact they'll outgrow their welcome and threaten pedestrians below. Why don't we go for a stroll and check out the competition?'

The AG and the GM amble along the street, surveying window boxes while the AG scans passing coats. They discover that, more often than not, windows are decked with window coffins not boxes, while a surprising number of passers-by sport dead sheep.

'Ericas dry out, as do lobelias,' says the GM, surveying yet another box of has-been heathers. 'Say what you like about scarlet geraniums, they're real survivors.'

Nevertheless, the AG sees a number of scarlet geraniums, sporting stalks like chicken legs and paltry flowers. She imagines the lives of those who have let their boxes go – the owners of the dead, the dying, the scraggy and the leafless. Maybe they planted for therapeutic purposes, which failed, leaving them too depressed to water. Maybe their lives are too full, too rich, too chaotic, too busy to permit plant care. The worst offenders are those with small, highly decorated, carefully-centred, terracotta window boxes. Those with the highest survival rate employ ordinary flowerpots filled with plants unidentifiable to the uninitiated. The AG's reflections are cut short by the sight of multi-coloured, tumbling petunias. She stops.

'Don't even think of it,' cries the GM, pulling her by the arm. 'Cascades are for banks and pubs. What's more, petunias are a hopelessly short-term investment. People who plant petunias regard their window boxes as cut flowers. You should treat your window box as a mini-nursery, stocked with stuff to be planted in the garden once it's done its stint on the sill.'

Like giving last year's coat to Oxfam, thinks the AG, although her garden has no room for plants regurgitated by the window boxes. 'So what should I plant?' she asks.

'Well, you need to decide on what profile you want; rising in the middle, popping up at either end, or set in a straight line. Don't go for jagged. You'll be forever pruning with your eyes. And you need to think whether you are planting for seduction or concealment. I mean, some people use window boxes as living net curtains. Be careful where cyclamen are concerned. Garden centres tend to sell them before they have hardened. Avoid anything with a face; it may emerge looking the wrong way. I'd keep it simple. Put in some bulbs like muscari and overplant with primulas or primroses.'

'It all sounds a bit Fortnum and Mason, double-breasted and belted. I was thinking fun fur,' sighs the AG.

'Go ahead, get your parka with fur round the hood, plant a fruit salad of pansies, asters, solanum, eunonymus, hebes, salvias, you name it. All you'll get is sequential collapse rather than simultaneous death, which is what you want in a window box. Think clifftop.'

The anxious gardener
fears for the future of her bulbs

The Anxious Gardener is ambivalent where bulbs are concerned. They are summer's full stops; their purchasing and planting ushers in autumn. On the other hand, a pot of bulbs prophesies resurrection and new beginnings – as long as the gardener follows the rules. Otherwise the promising womb will be a disappointing tomb.

The AG is committed to following rules but the instructions are contradictory. The good gardener buys bulbs early while stocks are plentiful and choice is ample, yet the good gardener mustn't leave the purchases lying around to grow sick and mildewed. But neither does the good gardener plant prematurely. Planting on time matters. Planting on time is unimportant; late planting simply means late arrivals.

'Your trouble,' says Maud-Next-Door, 'is that you believe everything you read. You need to trust your intuition. Personally, I never follow recipes.'

The AG, who never cooks without a cookery book to hand, is particularly troubled by tulips. Lilies, crocuses,

The Anxious Gardener is particularly troubled by tulips

daffodils and hyacinths need to go in during September and October but tulips must wait quietly until November 2nd and then be put in at speed before Guy Fawkes' night. 'Given that all bulbs live in the earth, why is there such a narrow window of opportunity for tulip planting?' she asks the Gardening Mentor.

'We're dealing here not with the natural order, but with natural disaster. I'm talking tulip fire. Leaving tulips until November when the soil is cooler lessens the risk of fungal disease. And put them in too early and they pop up prematurely, before the weather is ready for them.'

Tulip fire sounds rather fine to the AG.

'Think again. It's incurable. Your tulip turns brown, scorched and withered before rotting. The disease is in soil.'

'But then there's nothing to worry about!' exclaims the AG, uncharacteristically. 'My tulips are going in pots – in bulb fibre.'

'Don't tell me you've purchased bulb fibre! An unnecessary gimmick if ever there was one. Be sure to handle the bulbs carefully. They bruise. Plant them three times their own depth or you'll get premature floppy foliage. And make sure your drainage is adequate or you'll suffer incurable basal rot. And squeeze a bulb gently before buying it to make sure it's firm and healthy.'

'Anything else?'

'Protect against squirrels. Now, what I do . . .'

But the AG, impatient to go bulb shopping, stops listening.

Like pick 'n' mix sweets at Woolworths, bulbs are sold by the bagful. At the garden centre, eager gardeners are cramming bags greedily to breaking point. The AG joins in enthusiastically, captivated by the technicolour photographs of the plants-to-be, tacked up above the boxes of bulbs. Only once she has stuffed six bags does she remembers that bulbs are anonymous. Already she has forgotten which bag houses the pink tulips and which the red. She tips them back, labels her bags and starts again – only to commit another error. She wants a simultaneous display of maroon, cerise and dusty pink tulips, but the bulbs she's crammed into her bag are a mixture of early, middle and late tulips. No one told her that tulips are staggered over spring. She tips them out and starts again.

Back home, ruler in hand, she plants her bulbs with infinite care, layering tulips, daffodils and *Iris reticulata*. The process provokes considerable anxiety. Should the bulbs be touching or not? Will the tulips be able to make their way past first the daffodils and then the irises above their heads? Does it matter that she didn't scrub the pots before planting? How many bits of smashed terracotta should she place over the drainage holes?

'It's much the same as applying semi-permanent hair dye,' observes Maud-next-door. 'Ignore the instructions and just bung it on.'

The AG glances up at Maud and hurries indoors to phone the Gardening Mentor.

'The only thing that really, really matters is protecting the pots against squirrels. You have two and a half million bulb addicts waiting to get yours.

'And that's just grey squirrels. There are also one hundred and sixty thousand red squirrels. What's more, your timid squirrel is a thing of the past.'

'OK, so what am I to do?'

'Grating lemon soap on the surface of the pot works, but it doesn't do much for the appearance of the pot. Scattering chicken-manure pellets is successful but smelly. Applying chemical deterrents is inadvisable, not on ideological grounds, but because many squirrels just take them in their stride. Personally, I go for chicken wire cut to size, placed over the pot and tucked down the side of the pot under the compost, even though chicken wire is infuriating to cut and horribly hard to handle. I've heard say that a most effective deterrent is a two-centimetre layer of horticultural grit laid on the compost. But whatever you use, don't risk unprotected bulbs for even a night.'

Night is, indeed, falling along with a light rain. The AG has no wish to start struggling with chicken wire in such conditions. What is more she truly loves squirrels, with their magical tails, their agility and their able little paws. To be vandalised by a squirrel would be tantamount to being mauled by her own dog, she thinks and decides to wait until morning before squirrel proofing her pots.

The wages of procrastination is death of bulbs. Vandals strike. Next day, like pepper on a pizza, compost is scattered over the patio, and bulbs, with their white hearts ripped open, lie half-eaten at her feet. Even the pots have been knocked over and cracked in a desperate digging for the addictive substance. The Anxious Gardener knows her enemy. Tree rats, she thinks, tree rats with overblown tails.

The anxious gardener
makes excuses

Mary, a competent gardener, is calling to see the AG's garden. The prospect sends her anxiety levels way up, from productive to destructive. Her ability to judge her planting scheme turns into blanket condemnation of her beds. Feverishly, in anticipation of the visit, she dead-heads, snips, shifts, uproots and supports.

Her excuses flow from the moment she opens the door to her friend. Between a double kiss, she explains that the council had refused to allow her to take down the tree overhanging the front garden, which annually drops toxic sticky stuff on to her hapless plants. 'So you see that's why it looks so bare,' she concludes.

*A tall white tobacco plant appears to
be closely inspecting the garden path*

'But I adore that *Nicotiana sylvestris*,' says her friend, pointing to a tall white tobacco plant that appears to be closely inspecting the garden path. Of course the AG had intended to stake it 'but I just didn't have time,' she explains.

Stepping through the French windows to her back garden, the AG sees at once how one-note it is. And the note is green. She turns to Mary. 'Of course, at this time of year dahlias and asters and penstemon give a garden colour. But not mine. They'd hardly last a day with my snail problem. It's true they don't eat penstemon. I don't know what it is with me and penstemon.' She trails off.

Mary is reassuring. She praises the waving wands of *Verbena bonariensis*. She admires the purple spires of *Liriope muscari*. She waxes lyrical over a kaffir lily. But seemingly deaf, the AG soldiers on with her litany of excuses. 'I know there's a definite lack of blue,' she says, 'I just wish you could have come earlier while the morning glory was out and too bad the tradescantia's closed.'

Mary catches site of the rose 'Blush Noisette'. 'My absolute favourite rose! Such a star!' The AG jumps in quickly. 'Such a shame you didn't see it in July. It was quite amazing. The problem, though, with cluster flowered roses is that some flowers in the cluster turn brown before others and spoil the show.' She seizes a stem of 'Blush Noisette' to make her point.

'Shake it,' instructs Mary.

'Shake it?'

'Yes, then the faded blossoms fall and you're left with still perfect blooms.'

Gratefully the AG shakes the rose free of fading blooms until all that remains is perfection. Then the AG apologises for her previous ignorance of the technique, while anxiously following Mary's gaze until she thinks it lights upon a bare patch of earth.

'I know, I know,' cries the AG. 'Isn't it awful? Such a dank corner! What would you do with it? I've tried everything from anemones to dicentras. The only thing that agrees to grow there is wild borage. Yes, a pretty blue flower. I've just cut it back because, frankly, it was looking a mess. Something had been at its big leaves. And now look at it!'

Mary does, indeed, turn and look at the corner that had, until then, escaped her notice. Struggling to distract from the offending patch, the AG unfolds her future plans. She intends to have a blue 'Prince Charles' clematis, along with the purple clematis 'Polish Spirit' and the dark red 'Mme Julia Correvon', all set off nicely by the pink rose 'Clair Matin', which normally wouldn't climb. 'But because my garden is so miserably dark, it reaches for the light,' she adds hastily, aware that, compensating for inadequacy, she's sounding a touch grandiose.

'Should be lovely,' says Mary, 'The clematis are all late-flowerers and relatively easy.'

'You're right,' exclaims the AG. I should include a large-flowered spring blooming variety. The fireworks will all be late in the year, Oh dear! And that rose over there, that one, 'Marjorie Fair'; I should have pruned her harder.'

Mary stops and turns on the Anxious Gardener. 'Apology,' she says, 'is aggression in disguise.'

The anxious gardener
repulses an invader

On the party wall, outside the Anxious Gardener's kitchen window, she has planted a splendid climber – *Campsis* 'Mme Galen'. Every year, in late summer, it puts forth flowers that are the envy of all her friends. It is universally acclaimed – so exotic for North London, so gloriously redolent of holidays in Southern Europe. The AG receives the congratulations with appropriate modesty.

Secretly, however, she harbours disquiet about the climber. Undoubtedly Mme Galen eases the transition from holidays to homecoming, flowering as she does in late August. But the trumpets are orange. Although the AG looks back fondly on a long-lost orange mini-skirt, she can't abide the colour, with its distressing suggestion of marigolds. Season after season, Mme Galen's orange trumpets drown out the subtle colour scheme the AG struggles to achieve. And not only does Mme Galen shout down other more discreet late-flowerers, like *Anemone blanda*, but she competes violently with everything in sight, rampaging over the wall and winning resounding victories. So far she numbers three roses amongst her victims – strangled and suffocated.

The AG struggles to remain in control of the situation, fiercely cutting back the campsis almost to ground level every year. Undaunted, Mme Galen springs up and regains her former glory with ease. The AG has to admire her.

'If you want my advice, she's outgrown your garden,' remarks the Gardening Mentor.

The AG agrees – and disagrees. Mme Galen may be violent but she is so resilient, so reliable, so determined and fearless. She's a suffragette amongst climbers.

There is, however, a hint of trouble to come. The campsis starts to produce shoots liberally. The AG digs them up and gives them to grateful gardening friends. But quite quickly she runs out of friends. Supply way exceeds demand. Armies of little campsis appear. The faster the AG digs them up, the faster they shoot skywards.

It is during a supper of spaghetti that the AG realises that the campsis isn't simply engaged in reproduction but actually mounting an invasion. 'Mum,' cries her son, 'what's that?' At first, as the AG peers behind the radiator, she thinks a child has disposed of unwanted spaghetti. Slowly it dawns on her that she faces, not a string of pasta but an aetiolated shoot of campsis.

*Mme Galen's orange trumpets drown out the subtle
colour scheme the Anxious Gardener struggles to achieve*

'Ugh, gross,' exclaims her daughter.

Mme Galen had forced her way through the skirting board and is scaling the radiator with ease. The AG shares her children's disgust. The beautiful climber has metamorphosed into a sallow parasite.

'Day of Triffids. Come quick.' She texts the Gardening Mentor.

Emptying the dishwasher, the AG finds further evidence of Mme Galen's invasive tendencies. A white stalk peers round the corner of the machine. Opening the cutlery drawer reveals another forced entry. Any shred of remaining affection for Mme Galen evaporates. The plant has crossed the boundary from the Natural to the Unnatural.

Slamming the drawer on the intruder, she shouts, 'She's got to go. I can't take any more.'

Secateurs fuelled by fury, she is attacking the campsis when the Gardening Mentor arrives.

'You won't solve the problem that way. The more you cut back, the stronger the root system grows. And judging by the way it's invaded the kitchen, an unbeatable underground network has already been established. You need to check your damp course.'

The Anxious Gardener feels curiously unclean.

'I just want her out of there,' she cries.

'You'll have to poison her.'

'Poison?'

'Cut the climber down to the stump. Slip a few crystals of Dax into the stump, seal it and bye bye Mme Galen.'

'But what about wild life? The cats? The children?'

'Unless they get down on all paws and gnaw the stump, they'll come to no harm.'

'Could you do it for me? While I'm out?' asks the Anxious Gardener.

The anxious gardener
discovers change is possible

September sees the Anxious Gardener castigating herself for things she has done in the garden – or left undone. Clashing colours, awkward relationships and plants out of place offend the eye at every turn.

'What have I *not* done wrong?' she wails, suffused in self-hatred.

'Get moving,' snaps the Gardening Mentor, 'while the soil is still warm! If it upsets you, move it. Or at least start forward planning some shape shifting.'

The AG feels anxious indeed. She doesn't do moving. Moving on is a foreign concept to her. Moving up in the world is just asking to be shot down, moving on means separation and moving aside is humiliating. To move a plant that has consented to root, grow and flower for her sake seems little short of sacrilege. She says some of this to the GM.

'Find a fork,' comes the reply. 'Dig down deep on all sides of the plant then lever up gently. There's nothing to it so long as you take your time. Speed kills.'

The AG contemplates the possibility of repair and regeneration implicit in moving. The three red campanulas bowed down and suffocating beneath the weight of the rose 'Rosy Cushion' could be moved and provided with standing room. The pretty, pale mallow now obscuring two roses could be shifted to the end of the garden where it could flop and spread with impunity. The *Verbena bonariensis*, which has strayed to the front of a bed, could be put back where such a tall, waving plant belongs. Yet all could be lost in translation.

'Be honest, what is the mortality rate associated with moving?'

'I told you: take it slowly, dig deeply round the plant, prepare the new location well and, as long as you don't let the

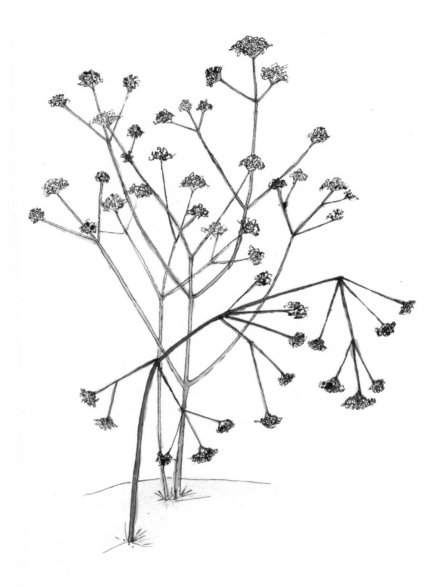

The verbena hangs its purple head in shock

roots dry out in transit, you'll have no loss of life.'

Maud-Next-Door, eavesdropping, starts to sing, 'Killing me softly . . .'

'Your point?' shouts the GM, approaching the trellis.

'Oh, nothing,' comes the disembodied reply. 'In fact I am pro-moving. Settling for a badly laid out garden, is trantamount to staying together for the sake of the children. Although you could argue that having made your bed you should lie in it.' She pauses, wanting laughter. 'Well, I can't stand here chatting idly all day.'

The AG and the GM listen in silence to her footsteps retreating up the garden path then abruptly halting. 'Incidentally,' she calls loudly, 'without wanting to be inhospitable, I would be more than grateful if you could move that bloody evergreen clematis that's clambering through on to my side of the trellis.'

The request exonerates the AG. She will be moving plants not simply to satisfy her narcissism but acting at the behest of others. She'll be obeying orders. If something should pass away in the process, she won't be to blame. She advances on the verbena, seizing a fork, preparing to relocate the wandering plant to the back of the bed where it belongs. She provides it with a generous home, deeply dug and furnished with well-rotted horse manure. Although she does her best to fork around the verbena, levering it out of the ground with enormous care, she hears with horror the sound of snapping roots. Battling to keep calm, she settles it in its new setting – and then panics. The verbena is hanging its purple head in shock.

'It's drooping!' she calls to the GM.

'Water well and wait,' comes the reply.

The AG comforts herself with the thought that the verbena was, anyway, soon due to be cut down in readiness for winter and the prospect of next year's replacement.

Meanwhile, she is finding moving unexpectedly satisfying. As she shifts her plants round the garden, she wishes that the features of her face or the location of her friends were equally amenable to change. 'Playing God,' she murmurs as she levers out a salvia, transports an aquilegia and firms the soil around a campanula.

Glancing up, she sees the verbena has recovered its poise and seems to have accepted its new position in life. Change, for the Anxious Gardener, stops signifying loss – sometimes.

The anxious gardener
lives to regret mail order

URGENT LIVE PLANTS. Loud red letters force the Anxious Gardener out into the wind and rain. UNPACK UPON ARRIVAL. She carries the large cardboard box to the garden, places it upon the wooden table and goes in search of scissors.

Excited at the prospect of the new arrivals, she begins to unpack the box. Hermetically sealed, it resists all attempts at penetration. Layers of broad brown sticky tape smother every orifice. The AG imagines she can hear parched plants within, crying for rain. Stabbing the scissors through the cardboard, she fears decapitating them. At last the wrappings give way, revealing layers of white Styrofoam balls, which the wind seizes and snows round the garden.

Greedily the AG inspects her purchases. Though somewhat crushed and desiccated, most still display green leaves. She lines up the little pots and exposes them to the rain. The plants are painfully, pitifully, small and fragile. Having become separated from their labels, many are now utterly anonymous. The order form lies crumpled, soaked and illegible at her feet.

Months had passed since AG had filled in the mail order form. The catalogue had enticed her with promises of long flowering periods, delicious fragrance, enchanting colour

*Looking at the delicate green foliage the Anxious Gardener
remembers supporting her babies' heads before their necks
were strong enough to do the job unaided*

combinations, thriving in any good garden soil. Desire and caution had done battle for her soul. No contest. She had made out a hefty cheque for plants known only from seductive photographs, ignoring in guilt-ridden haste the small print, which warned 'young plants prefer 3–4 weeks in pots before being planted'.

Some of the nurslings have held on to their labels. She seizes a viola and identifies six more. Why had she purchased violas? What wording in the catalogue had convinced her that she needed six violas? Where had she proposed to plant them? Wet and worried, she manages to assemble little groups of mallows, campanulas, omphalodes, penstemon and *Iris pallida* 'Variegata'. All of them tiny, all of them needing nursing before facing the rigours of the open garden.

'To be honest,' says the Gardening Mentor that evening on the phone, 'even if they survive, you're unlikely to see flowers on them this year. Well, the violas might flower but you'll be lucky to see a penstemon. Given your levels of anxiety, never purchase anything smaller than a five-litre pot, which is what you get in garden centres. Forget plugs and steer clear of two-litre pots. Catalogues require cynical handling. And don't throw them out after you've placed the order. And always keep a copy of the order form. You never know whether you've been sent what you ordered. I well remember ordering asters and receiving *Hesperis matrolanis*. By the time the bloody things had come up, I had *Hesperis* seeding everywhere . . .'

'So what am I to do with them?' the AG interrupts, knowing that the GM has to be reined forcibly to the gardening point. She gazes out of the window at the little cluster of pots with their tiny occupants. 'They do look as if they are enjoying the rain.'

'You've left them out in the rain! All their lives they've been nurtured in greenhouses, or polytunnels, under lights, with heating. Bring them in now and call me back.'

The AG hurries into the wind and rain, retrieves the pots. They drip onto the kitchen floor. Looking at the delicate green foliage, she is reminded of supporting her babies heads before their necks were strong enough to do the job unaided.

'Now what?' she says into the phone.

'Fresh compost, clean pots and keep them in a good light. Don't let them get cold and pick off any brown and mouldy bits. And don't worry if any have flopped. Plants are much tougher than we think.'

'How can you recommend twenty-four nursing and then tell me that plants are much tougher than we think!'

She knows she's not about to rig up heat and light for the babies. Her efforts on behalf of her plants fuse at a certain point. She worries to the point of short-circuiting her system; inertia and corner-cutting then take over.

'You lot are just going to have to survive beneath the garden bench as best you can,' she says to the tiny new arrivals. Then suddenly she regrets her parsimonious order. She should have completely thrown caution to the winds and purchased a dozen violas, and as many penstemon and twice the number of campanulas, maybe ten Iceland poppies and those lovely red salvias and forget-me-nots, which, after all, seed themselves. Then she could have afforded to lose some to hypothermia. Only guilt at profligacy prevents a glorious garden.

The anxious gardener
is perplexed by planting

The Anxious Gardener decides the time has come to plant out the purchases. It may be premature but she can no longer bear the sight of them waiting for freedom. Some look ill and she hopes that fresh soil and the possibility of expansion will provide them with a new lease of life.

She picks up the pots and positions them round the garden. Carefully she places them in order of height and their relative need for sunlight or shade. Once all are sitting comfortably, though slightly askew upon the earth, she stands back and surveys the beds. Manic happiness seizes the AG. Of course, she can no longer remember the colour of the plants purchased cavalierly from catalogues but she can foresee a bounteous garden. The little plants will stretch their roots and grow. And nothing is yet set in stone. She potters happily, moving a campanula, adjusting the position of a penstemon, and lifting a viola forward to edge a bed.

Armed with trowel and compost, the AG digs the first hole – for a mallow. It promises to be bushy, tall and quite partial to partial shade. She places it where it will do a good cosmetic job, concealing legginess so regrettable in a rose and so entirely her own fault. If only she had had the guts to prune hard. But she's always shied away from cosmetic surgery, and like an ageing face, roses grow leggy surreptitiously until suddenly it's too late to do anything about it. The mallow will, however, be a fine concealer.

It's then that the doubts set in. If she digs too close to the rose, she might disturb a root; sever it even. And what if she digs too deep and the surface of the pot sinks beneath the level of the soil. She's heard that's potentially disastrous but she has no clue why. And should she surround the plant with new compost or leave it to become acquainted with the resident soil?

Then there's the question of bone meal. Gardening books instruct her to enrich the soil with a good handful of bone meal. But when a neighbour obeyed and planted with bone meal, she emerged next day to find her new babies flung around the garden. A starving urban fox, convinced a delicious kill lay beneath the soil, had dug frantically. The AG decides to stick to artificial fertiliser. She is, anyway, particularly anxious around bone meal. Whose bones, she wonders,

The plant will conceal the legginess so
regrettable in a rose and so entirely her own fault

and what was the cause of death. She will stick to Growmore. But where should she sprinkle it? Beneath, beside or above the plant? And how much is a handful? And what if she exceeds the dose?

Shaking the soil from her trowel, she goes indoors and phones the Gardening Mentor with the package of planting worries.

'It's premature to plant out now. We're only in February. I'd treat them as bedding plants and put them out in May.'

The AG tries to explain that it's akin to addiction. She has started planting and can't stop.

'OK, but the wisest thing would have been to put the pot in the ground just to start them off. Undisturbed they can grow accustomed to their new surroundings. You could leave them for up to three months in their pots.'

'And when they are sufficiently well-adjusted to face the rigours of the soil, do I put in fresh compost or introduce them to the local stuff?'

'That's easy. Mix the existing soil with fresh compost to boost it. Don't get too agitated about depth of planting. Just make sure the crown of the plant is above the soil or it'll rot, particularly with primroses. Now I was planting primroses quite recently and . . .'

'Actually, we're not talking primroses,' interjects the AG, anticipating an unwanted flood of primrose narratives. 'What about food?'

'To be honest, in my view, you've blown it with Growmore. It's too strong for roots. I would never put Growmore in the bottom of a hole. It can burn roots. Use blood, fish and bone.'

'Foxes!' wails the AG.

'Point taken. So plant them, water them and then soak the root ball with Miracle-Gro which is high in phosphorus that promotes root growth. Only the other day, someone was saying to me that they used Phostrogen or Tomorite. I said,

"That's all very well for flower growth; they're fertilisers high in potassium which promotes *flower growth* but what you're wanting when planting is *root growth*, for God's sake!" Of course, for planting, you can use bonemeal, which contains phosphorus, but phosphorus isn't very mobile. Put bonemeal in the bottom of a hole and it sinks down. There's an argument for bonemeal on top.'

'Foxes,' says the AG wearily. 'I told you that I can't use bonemeal. And what if I apply more than a handful of fertiliser?'

'Well, a handful equals an ounce or twenty-seven grams. If you exceed the dose of a slow release fertiliser it's less of a problem than a quick fertiliser, although even then you may burn the roots. That's the main problem. Or if you use too much nitrogen you'll promote excessive growth. You'll have saggy, leggy plants, green and mouldy. I don't think there's a problem if you exceed the dose of phosphorus because, as I said, it's not very mobile in the soil. Or potassium. But really it depends upon the time of year . . .'

The names of chemical compounds have a curiously anaesthetizing effect on the AG. She tunes out, hangs up the phone and returns to the scene of the planting.

Fresh worries all too soon assail her. She knows she must firm the soil around the newly planted. But how firm is firm? Will she suffocate the little thing if she firms it with her foot? Will it suffer wind rock if she packs it in too loosely? Or do only tall plants suffer wind rock? Torn between the desire to achieve the perfect planting and the embarrassment of phoning the GM with further foolish questions, the AG goes for moderate firmness, patting the soil surrounding the new arrival as if preparing pastry for rolling.

At last each new plant is in its new home, side by side with a white spatula of a label bearing its name. Tired and deeply satisfied, the AG sinks into a garden chair and surveys the beds, spotted with new arrivals. The sun emerges from a cloud just as the AG's cat emerges from the house. The freshly turned earth beckons. The garden has become one large and welcoming litter tray. Enthusiastically the cat digs, displacing a viola. Carefully the cat covers its traces, decapitating a campanula. The Anxious Gardener watches in despair, devotion to cats doing battle with passion for plants.

The anxious gardener
longs for the unobtainable

The Anxious Gardener blames the television gardening programme. Normally she finds it therapeutic. Issuing clear instructions, providing succinct advance warnings, it allays her horticultural doubts and fears. Looking back she's not sure which moment set up her longing for a pond. It could have been the repeated footage of one presenter donning thigh-high waders and plunging into yet another water feature, or the other presenter informing viewers that the pleasure of ponds was 'just looking', as the camera played across his features, gazing into space. Or maybe it was the delightful clutch of ducks, bobbing on the tele-made pond. One way or another the damage was done and her garden seemed suddenly a dry land devoid of pleasing water.

'I want one,' she said aloud to the screen as lack created desire.

'Children can drown in only two inches of water,' warns her mother.

'It'll be breeding ground for mosquitoes, and given global warming, they'll soon be malarial,' says her daughter.

'How can you consider indulging in a pond at a time of water shortage?' cries her son.

Like a dieter deprived of chocolate, she can think of nothing but her pond

Listening to the massed anxious objections, the AG reflects on the genetic roots of anxious gardening. But still she longs for a pond. Fighting for her water feature, she argues on behalf its ecological advantages. It will provide a breeding ground for beneficial insects. It will offer a bath to the birds. She doesn't add that it will also offer her an opportunity to plant all sorts of moisture-loving plants, at present way beyond the means of her dehydrated plot.

'And fish!' she exclaims enthusiastically. 'We could have fish and water boatmen and newts and tadpoles.'

'Cats!' chorus her family. 'And really it's like having a dog in London; hard work, time consuming and unnatural.'

Like a dieter deprived of chocolates, she can think of nothing but her pond, fringed with reeds and floating with lilies while dark shapes slip beneath the surface.

'So many people have ponds,' she says to her gardening friend, Mary, proud owner of a mature pond, 'Why not me?'

'To be honest,' replies her friend, 'the potential to sink into guilt in a pond is always there. It's not plain sailing.' She gives a deprecatory laugh. 'Seriously, the liner can split or rot, leaving fish and vegetation literally gasping, Blanket weed can choke and smother. Leaves never leave a pond alone. The sun can dry and desiccate. The water can leach away into the lawn. Seriously, have you the ego strength?'

Uncertain as to the meaning of ego strength, the AG is nevertheless sure she must lack it. So now, at the first hint of water, the Anxious Gardener averts her eyes from television gardening programmes. A presenter in waders is a sign for her to go and make tea.

The anxious gardener
struggles with a rose sucker

The Anxious Gardener is religiously removing hips from the tall canes of her rugosa rose. A handsome plant called 'Hansa', it rewards her diligence by producing large untidy magenta flowers even in August. She's heard that producing hips exhausts a rose and she is fond of Hansa. So, at the first hint of a hip, she speedily snips down as far as the first responsible-looking leaf. She knows hips 'provide autumn colour' but it's flowers she hungers for.

She's mid-snip when she spies the intruder. There in the heart of Hansa waves an alien wand. Knowing a sucker when she sees one, heart beating, the AG fearfully inspects the parasite. Whereas Hansa's stalks are speckled with prickles, the intruder's stalks are smooth. Hansa's leaves are pale and somewhat crinkled. The intruder's leaves are dull and forthright. Thin and wiry, it waves flowerless above the rest of the rose bush.

'It's like a computer virus,' says the Gardening Mentor, 'that destroys the hard drive. Remove it or it will erase the rose entirely.'

'How?'

'Strip it out.'

'Strip?'

'Absolutely. Take hold of it and strip it away from the root. Wear gloves and goggles.'

Gloves on, the AG fights her way to the heart of the five-foot-high, five-foot-wide rose shrub. She locates the smooth stem of the sucker, grasps, pulls, yanks, heaves. The sucker remains resolutely attached to the root of the rose. Moreover, Hansa takes up the fight on behalf of the sucker; thorns tangle painfully in her hair and sink into the flesh of her arm. Blood stains her T-shirt.

In the heart of the rose 'Hansa' waves an alien wand

'It's for your own good,' she says to the rose as she bends and grasps a shorter, weaker sucker. Though she pulls with every bit of strength in her body, the sucker refuses to detach. It simply bends and bows beneath her hands. Hot and bleeding, she returns to the phone. 'They won't come away,' she bleats. 'How about if I cut them down?' 'Disastrous,' replies the GM. 'Cutting will simply encourage them. You know, like hair, if you cut it, it grows faster.' 'That's a myth,' replies the AG. 'It just seems to grow faster if you cut it.' 'Have it your way. You could decide that fate is decreeing you have a dog rose instead of rugosa. Because that's what you'll get when the takeover is complete. It's infanticide. The rugosa's parent is eating it alive. Think of rabbits. If you disturb a doe, she eats her babies.' 'But I haven't disturbed Hansa. I've done everything for that rose. I feed, dead-head, water. No rose could have been treated with greater consideration.' 'Basically, you've lacked vigilance. A good gardener maintains ceaseless vigilance. Had you inspected that rose every day, you could have spotted the sucker when it was nothing more than a little red bud starting below the graft, and you could have rubbed it out. As it is, you could try cutting the suckers from the root.' Returning to the scene of the crime, the AG visualizes fighting off the outraged rose as she digs down to locate the juncture of root and sucker. The Medea-mother, meanwhile, waves nonchalantly in the wind above her threatened progeny. 'What the eye doesn't see, the heart doesn't grieve over,' declares the Anxious Gardener and advances on Hansa. Smartly she seizes a sucker; smoothly she snips the stalk of the invasive mother. The alien wand falls from sight. And sadly, in the months to come, so does Hansa, swamped by suckers.

The anxious gardener
needs space

The Anxious Gardener divides plants and friends into the withholding and the invasive, into those who give too much and those who offer too little. *Lithodora* 'Heavenly Blue' gives too much and demands altogether too much space. The low spreading evergreen plant is metaphorically forever on the phone to her. It occupies a good third of a raised bed, cascading towards the patio, smothering all competitors.

'I wouldn't begrudge it the space if my garden was larger. Just as I wouldn't deny an importunate friend if I had the time at my disposal,' sighs the AG.

She and the Gardening Mentor inspect the dense matt of spiky shoots. With beautiful blue flowers, as the gardening books say, it brightens the spring but for the rest of the year she faces a dull, ever-spreading mat. She lifts a handful to reveal the dense, blackened foliage beneath.

'You never know what lies beneath the surface,' says the GM sagely.

'Like the rest of us,' answers the AG. 'But I'm feeling crowded by it. And it's limiting my options. I know I should be grateful that it deigns to grow so healthily, but . . .'

'You're supposed to be able to "cut back as required" says the GM. 'But in my experience lithodora is a sensitive flower; a hard winter, a hard cut back and that's it. No lithodora. No fine blue flowers in spring. Just be careful. Lay down a boundary; don't perform an execution.'

'Laying down a boundary is tantamount to dumping, you know it is,' The AG is growing worried. Given her ambivalent feelings towards the plant, how easy would it be to deliver a few poorly placed snips, putting an end to the relationship. She doesn't trust herself.

She peers at the plant and identifies the flowers it's recently

The low-growing evergreen is metaphorically forever on the phone to her

run down; a geranium and a dianthus that didn't stand a chance in its path. But something is fighting back. Thrusting up through the lithodora is a plant she'd forgotten planting whose name escapes her. A ground-cover plant (why didn't she keep the label?) with small mauve, late season, trumpet-like flowers is literally growing through the lithodora, propagated and protected by the other plant's presence

'Oh God, I can't possibly touch the lithodora; it would be like putting down a pregnant cat,' cries the AG, deciding at once on a stay of execution.

'Laying down a boundary with a pregnant cat?'

'Impossible. They always give birth on the duvet.'

The anxious gardener
has doubts about mulching

Initially the prospect of mulching satisfies the Anxious Gardener. The garden will be covered with a nutritious blanket of mushroom compost. All the guilt-inducing areas of neglect will sink from sight beneath the beneficial mulch. The uneven spots will be smoothed, the stony patches concealed, the poorly dug spots hidden from view. The AG is reminded of the pleasures of wearing a kaftan.

Other forms of feeding tend to worry the AG. When she wields the watering can to foliar feed, she worries about the imminence of rain washing off the nutrients. When she scatters granular feed, she finds herself wondering what the grey granules are made of. Once she inhaled a lungful of rose food and spent some time tensely anticipating the after-effects. Feeding individual plants reminds her of the precision and high standard expected of dinner parties while mulching is much the same as throwing a big Sunday lunch – maximum nourishment with minimum effort. All

'Oh my God,' exclaims the AG. 'If the mulch
suppresses the weeds what else will it suffocate?'

she has to do is spread two inches of mulch over the beds. A nice organic mulch, spread democratically over the garden, is tantamount to a generous, philanthropic gesture. Horse manure would, of course, be a different matter. She has read of the dangers of horse manure and farmyard manure. One scratch from a rose fed on horse manure can be fatal, or so she's been told. The cause of the fatality has slipped her mind but she's playing safe and opting for a vegetarian mulch. Then all of a sudden she recalls a mushroom compost warning issued by a television garden programme presenter. The leaves of roses turn a disagreeable shade of yellow if nurtured on mushroom compost. She hurries to the phone.

'Mushroom compost,' she says to the Gardening Mentor, 'does it disagree with roses?'

'Yellowing leaves suggest nutrient deficiency. In the case of the mushroom compost, it may be making the soil too alkaline. Anyway it's no good on ericaceous plants. And it'll turn your hydrangea pink. You need to bear in mind that the pH has to be right for the plants you're mulching around. To be frank, I stick to Gem – recycled garden compost. Smells pleasantly of pine,' answers the GM but in the tone of one coping with an unwelcome interruption.

The AG hears that she's on her own with this one. She weighs the pros and cons. A good mulch conserves water. The earth is now damp. The mulch will stop evaporation. The mulch will feed the plants during the growing season. The mulch will give the garden a lovely, healthy skin, almost airbrushed in its pleasing uniformity. And – a clinching factor – the mulch will suppress weeds.

'Oh my God,' exclaims the AG. If the mulch suppresses weeds what else will it suffocate? What seeds will it bury alive. What low-lying plants will be hidden from the sun beneath the regulation two inches of compost? She's poised to provide not a safety blanket but a shroud.

'Look, I'm really, really sorry to bother you, but you know I said I was worried about the mushroom compost, do you think there's a danger of it smothering small things?'

'Plants are programmed to push through earth. And as for seeds. Well, you should be mulching in the early spring or late autumn after the leaves have dropped and way before you plant seeds. Where is your basic trust? Gardeners have been mulching for centuries and now suddenly *you* see it as an instrument of death!'

'But what about self-seeders? I can't set their biological clock and control their timing! They may be poised to sprout only to be crushed beneath two inches of impenetrable muck?'

'If you mulch at the right time, when the self-seeders get going, the mulch will be well watered and no longer strong enough to burn the seed.'

'Bad timing will burn them?'

'Their timing? What about my time?'

It's rare indeed for the Gardening Mentor to manifest impatience in the face of her cries for help. Chastened, the AG mulches. But once the garden is covered in compost she finds a small stick. It's all very well to say that plants are programmed to push through soil, but what if they've already broken the surface, keen to face the sun, only to find soil showered down upon them. Imagining their discouragement and exhaustion, methodically she cleans compost from the bright, fragile leaves of newborn plants.

The anxious gardener
grows concerned about clematis

In late winter, tearing the tangled brown twigs from the trellis and cutting the plant down to nine inches above the ground satisfies the Anxious Gardener's desire for order and tidiness. Decluttering lightens the heart, she thinks, as she sweeps up the snappish remains of the clematis. Grey stumps stand where the clematis had scrambled up the trellis. Dry and bare, they are all that remains of the vigorous, small-flowered, purple viticella clematis, 'Polish Spirit'. Will it rise again? Guilt sets in. She has decimated the plant that has grown so profusely for her benefit. Then she recalls how it had rushed headlong over the trellis, deserting her in favour of her neighbour. The harsh treatment was well deserved. It would be a good while before the grounded plant left home again. But the worries won't be silenced.

'I haven't simply reduced it to a bud, I've hacked it right back to the grey lifeless bits,' she confesses to the Gardening Mentor.

'Have faith. By March or maybe even earlier, you'll start to see shoots. In fact it might have been a good thing to have cut it right down to the earth. We're talking viticellas here, not your hypersensitive large-flowered hybrids. Just make sure you manure it after cutting it back – like a nice cup of tea following a shock.'

'I worry that if I cut it right down to the ground something might eat it, or shit on it, or sit on it just as it reaches the light.'

'Just trust in grey stumps. But if it'll make you feel better, tie a bit of string around a grey stump and attach it to the trellis. That way when the new shoots appear, they'll have a highway to heaven waiting for them.'

The AG returns to the fray. She has two more clematis left

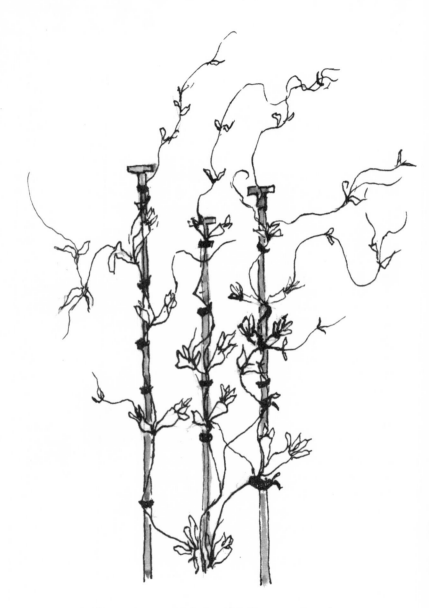

Barbara Harrington's brown brittle stems, though plastered to her bamboo, are showing signs of life

in need of treatment. These are new arrivals in her garden. They had been on irresistibly special offer in Columbia Road market. She had planted them along with their supportive canes in the earth about a foot and half below the trellis. Ever since she became a gardener she has suffered uncertainty in relation to the support system bearing up newly arrived clematis. She has never known whether to leave the plant chained to its bamboo or whether to set it free and risk rendering it deeply insecure. She had suffered much the same anxiety when faced with allowing the children to travel to school by themselves.

Standing gazing at the dark red 'Barbara Harrington' she sees that her brown brittle stems, though plastered to her bamboo, are showing signs of life. Slender green shoots are making bids for freedom but into thin air. Too short to reach the trellis, they nevertheless can't wait to escape the bamboo. A couple are even breaking cover at the foot of the bamboo. The AG is filled with optimism. She had planted Barbara Harrington next to the rose 'Blush Noisette', imagining the dark red clematis mingling happily with the white-pink rose flowers. But both the rose and the trellis are way beyond the grasp of Barbara's new shoots. Should she risk separating the clematis from its support, snipping the tight plastic ties? Will it simply slump to the foot of the bamboo?

Matters are more serious with the oddly named 'Blekitny Aniol' planted to complement the bright pink climbing China rose, 'Felemberg'. Of course, the Anxious Gardener has her doubts about Felemberg. Would she be seen as someone who rated a harsh pink rose? But Felemberg is so tough, so continuously in flower. And the blue clematis tangling in its arms would suggest that planting the rose had been an aesthetic choice, not simply a safe option. Anyway, she reminds herself, it shouldn't matter what other people think – the issue is the state of the poor blue clematis. Not even the suggestion of a fat bud or hint of green enlivens the brown twigs taped so securely to the bamboo. Was it dead or sluggish? Was it being strangled by green tape? Should she cut it down or throw it out?

'Tricky one,' says the GM. 'Have you snapped a bit off to see if it's green inside?'

'I was afraid of snapping off its one living limb.'

'Well, in the circumstances, cut it down, wait and see.'

'On the subject of clematis,' the AG continues, 'when should I detach new clematis from the bamboos they come with?'

'Leave it on the bamboo until it's found its way to the trellis. Side shoots will grow and wave around until they locate the trellis. As I said, you could tie a bit of string onto the trellis and let it dangle within reach of the clematis, so it can give itself a leg up. Your trouble is that you lack basic trust.'

She thinks she hears a sigh at the other end of the line.

SPRING

Like a free gift, a feral violet arrived in her garden

The anxious gardener
falls victim to violets

The Anxious Gardener can't recall what the dove carried in its beak when it returned to the ark to inform Noah that the flood waters were receding, but she considers it should have been the heart-shaped leaf of a violet. It's her favourite seasonal sign, declaring the end of winter and the onset of spring. Other such signifiers are vicious and prickly like mahonias or noisy and crowded like daffodils. Violets are discreet. Violets are subtle and she loves them.

When, like a free gift, a feral violet arrived in her garden, she felt deeply flattered. Although, looking back, she acknowledges that kitsch rhymes immediately came to mind:

> Roses are red
> Violets are blue
> Sugar is sweet
> And so are you

The immediate association might have warned her of what was to come. But at the time she merely reflected upon the fact that violets were not blue but a gentle purple, a colour she particularly prized.

The following spring, violets signified the season from all over the garden, between paving stones, in walls, ringing roses, practically astride aquilegias, thrusting up amongst geraniums. The AG remained delighted with her free gifts, which without a move on her part, were providing pleasing structural echoes across the beds.

It was another year before she realised that the violets were not just visiting but colonising. They were literally everywhere, oppressing the residents and utilizing precious resources.

'It's just so painful to love and hate the same object,' she cries to the Gardening Mentor. 'And I feel so politically reprehensible, as if I were raising paranoid objections to asylum seekers.'

'Funnily enough I thought the same thing about the baby last night. Fortunately you can dig up and dispose of the violets.'

But the AG can no more dig up and dispose of a violet than a baby. Maud-Next-Door, seeing her standing fork limply in her hand, trills Oscar Wilde through the trellis: 'Yet each man kills the thing he loves.'

'It's them or you,' warns the GM, while love and hate, life and death do battle for the AG's soul.

'I can't!' she says, letting fall the fork upon the faux-Yorkstone of the patio.

The GM retrieves it, gazes around the violet-clad garden, and is inspired. 'Look, think of them as feral cats persecuting the homegrown moggies.'

With those words, the violets assume a dramatically different complexion. Conflict resolves. Guilt and grief drain away. It's not the AG who is persecuting the violets, she is their hapless victim. No longer the sweet harbingers of spring, suddenly they convey the cloying sweetness of Parma Violets.

The anxious gardener
gives up on grass

'Your lawn, it resembles one of those counters in a children's game,' declares Maud-Next-Door. 'What's the name of the game? It begins with D. Not draughts, not dice . . .'

'Dominoes,' snarls the Anxious Gardener. Her beautiful lawn is, indeed, pitted with black holes reminiscent of the markings on a domino, signalling not one or even three but the number six. The lawn has become a feline public convenience. Cats come from miles around to use it; everyone else gives it a wide birth.

'That's really rank, Mum,' exclaims her daughter surveying the grass.

The AG had dreamed of a lawn with a nice stripe and a straight, well-defined edge; instead she has a litter tray. Resentfully she scatters compost over the holes and reseeds the offending spots with the Gardening Mentor's warnings ringing in her ears: 'Don't overseed. It only creates competition, which leads to die-off and rotting. Don't forget a bird deterrent. I hang CDs that rotate and flash in the sunlight. Put chicken wire over the reseeded areas and don't panic.'

Once all is reseeded, hung with CDs and clothed in chicken wire, the AG feels a satisfaction akin to having changed a dirty sheet or a soiled nappy. But overnight the cats return, and claw their convenience free of chicken wire. They are creatures of habit. The AG is reminded of insomnia. Just two nights of waking at two and the habit becomes unbreakable.

'Try returfing.' advises the Gardening Mentor. 'But for God's sake, make sure you buy good quality turf. You don't want hot sweaty grass with black bits and yellow slime. You mustn't worry if the turf starts off looking good and then gets manky. It'll soon look good again. Turf has a natural cycle.'

The cats swiftly interrupt the natural cycle. Turf flies beneath their paws.

'You've closed the stable door after the horse has bolted,' comments the GM, thoughtfully.

'We're talking cats not horses, lawn not pasture,' snaps the AG, who is becoming increasingly distraught at losing control of her lawn.

'Keep your hair on, or should I say turf. Seriously, you must render the lawn repulsive to cats before attempting repair. The shelves at the garden centre are groaning with anti-cat ammunition.'

Overnight the cats return and claw their convenience free of chicken wire

The AG does, indeed find a wealth of cat repellent, but each smells worse than the last. Get Off My Garden smells of rotting lemons. Renardine reminds her of Jeyes fluid. Growing Success stinks of garlic. Then there is Roar, which consists of expanded clay soaked in lion's urine, and Zoo Poo – granulated lion's shit. Far from frightening the cats, lion's excrement incites them to mark their territory with ever increasing zeal.

'Personally, I favour a cat scarer,' remarks the GM. 'Most of them give off a permanent ringing sound, a garden variety of tinnitus. But for two hundred pounds you can obtain one that only rings intermittently.'

The AG decides that given the alternatives, there is no alternative but to part with the lawn. The GM digs up the lawn while she is out to save her feelings and suggests that a time capsule be buried beneath the new faux-York-stone patio that is to take the place of the lawn. The children favour enclosing photos of the cats, CDs, and a video of *Breakfast at Tiffany's* but the AG insists on photos of the lawn instead.

After the lawn has gone, the AG is reminded how she felt when the children's lizards left home. The palpable relief of no longer feeding insects to reptiles was comparable to the release she now feels at having no grass to mow. Mowing, she finally realizes, is a sadomasochistic practice. No longer would she mow over frogs, faeces and worms. No longer would stones and garden wire tangle with the mower. No longer would she anticipate electrocution as she mowed through the machine's flex. Contentedly she sweeps clean her new faux-York-stone.

The anxious gardener
manages parthenogenesis

Given the soaring death-rate in her garden, the Anxious Gardener is particularly grateful to the survivors. *Iris sibirica* is a star in this respect. Every autumn she shears the sword-like foliage and every spring, from amongst the ragged, brown leavings, come fresh new shoots.

It's a bright spring morning when she sees with pain that the iris has lost heart. 'There's this big bald patch at the heart of the plant,' she wails down the phone to the Gardening Mentor. 'It's come up in a circle like some goddamn fairy mushroom ring. The one plant I could rely on to make me feel an effective gardener, the only plant that shored up my self-respect, and this happens. I'm tempted to chuck in the trowel.'

'Self-pity doesn't suit you. What's happened is perfectly natural.'

'As is self-pity.'

'Think of macular degeneration,' continues the GM. 'It's an old plant and it degenerates from the centre, just like your eyes.'

'Nothing can be done about macular degeneration,' says the AG stiffly.

'That's where you're wrong. I've heard that bilberry and lutein work wonders. And as for the iris, all you have to do is lift and divide.'

To the AG 'lift and divide' has the ring of an instruction barked out at the gym, rather than an action appropriate to gardening.

'And co-incidentally there's a feature on lift and divide in today's *Telegraph*.'

The AG smuggles the *Telegraph* into the garden, keeping it well away from hard-line, left-leaning children. Not only is

She understands the dynamics of violence as affection for the iris
evaporates and it becomes, in her eyes, an undeserving victim

there a feature on lifting and dividing but there are also surgical close-ups of plants being torn apart at the roots. The AG
looks sadly at the iris. Should it too be rewarded for its loyal-
ty and fidelity by being dug up and broken in half? Maybe
she should allow nature to take its course and let it vanish
from the centre out?

'There's nothing natural about lifting and dividing,' she
says to the GM.

'There's nothing natural about taking bilberry and lutein
for the eyes,' replies the GM, thoughts still on supplements,
'or statins for cholesterol or calcium for thinning bones.
You'll be giving the old thing a new lease of life.'

Persuaded, spade in hand, the AG descends upon the iris.
She thrusts the spade into the soil at a respectful distance, on
all sides of the plant. She digs deep and levers from below.
The iris remains unmoved. She prods, nudges and lifts. The
iris stays deeply attached to the ground. Hot and frustrated,
the AG grabs the plant and pulls. 'Five, four, three, two one,
lift-off!' she cries as the iris leaves the earth.

Having achieved lift-off, she still has to divide.

'Couldn't I just take a carving knife to the roots,' she asks
the GM.

'And sever a main artery? No, all you have to do is take
two forks.'

'I don't have two forks, for God's sake.'

'Nip next door and borrow Maud's. Then plunge the two
forks back to back into the root ball and gently pull them
apart.'

It sounds so easy on paper. But even the illustrated guide
provided by the *Telegraph* is no help. The GM struggles with
clashing forks and tangled roots, mangling the poor iris in
the process. She understands the dynamics of violence as
affection for the iris evaporates and, in her eyes, it becomes
nothing more than a recalcitrant, undeserving victim. Finally
it falls in half.

'Chuck out the damaged bits and pieces,' orders the GM.

'The whole thing looks like damaged goods to me,' answers the AG.

'You're overwrought. Just replant the best bits and give them a good feed.'

Neatly planted and well fed, with no nasty naked patches at their hearts, the two new irises look none the worse for parthenogenesis.

'Twins,' she says, delighted to the GM.

'Loaves and fishes,' comes the reply.

The anxious gardener
sows the seeds of desire

Growers from seed occupy the moral high ground of the garden, looking down on those who buy ready-made plants. They liken the latter to profligate consumers of takeaways. Growers from seed, on the other hand, are the home cooks of the gardening world. That's how the Anxious Gardener sees it. But even amongst the growers from seed there's a pecking order. At the pinnacle sit the growers from seed gathered at holiday destinations. They are wont to open their refrigerators and proudly display small, carefully sealed packets, labelled, for example, 'Tagetes, Honfleur, 2001' or '*Althaea niger*, Nice, 2000'. Gazing at the packets, the AG is reminded of her local swimming pool. Overtaken by someone in the fast lane provokes no pang, because the swimmer speeding past is well beyond the margins of her envy. She can't compete.

One day, however, she was admiring her friend Mary's cornflowers: pink, purple, red and blue cornflowers growing in profusion. 'Oh, I've heaps more seeds in the fridge,' said Mary, 'far more than I can use.' The AG declined the gift

Growers from seed occupy the moral high ground of the garden

explaining that she lacked the moral fibre and nerves of steel required of a grower from seed.

'Don't be such a weed!' exclaimed Mary, laughing in a rather irritating manner at her own gardening joke. 'It's so deeply satisfying. It's like extreme skiing. Once you've skied off-piste, you can't imagine ever again leaving fresh snow for the beaten track.'

The AG thinks it rather an apt comparison. Fresh, unmarked snow scares her and fills her with nameless dread. Who knows what's concealed beneath the surface? Growing from seed in a smooth tilth, suggests the same confrontation with the concealed and the unknown. But her friend is insistent. She presses a little white packet of cornflower seeds on the AG, who tucks it at the back of her fridge along with abandoned jars and tubes labelled 'refrigerate after opening'.

It's March when she spring cleans the fridge and comes upon the packet. Her garden is still bare but displaying signs of potential which gives her confidence. She decides it's time she sampled the courage and superior pleasures of growing from seed.

'Are you sure you want to go down this road?' asks the Gardening Mentor. 'You know how easily nervous you get. It won't just be foxes, cats, slugs and shuttlecocks opposing you. There'll be the birds.'

The AG envisages the birds who live in her garden: three blackbirds, the robin and the pairs of bluetits, swooping enthusiastically upon her seeds. Then suddenly she sees a solution.

'You know the big tub with the *Trachelospermum jasminoides*? I could scatter the cornflower seeds on the surface and protect them with chicken wire. Should I cover them with soil or leave them sitting on the surface?'

'Sow them thinly and lightly, covering them with maybe half an inch of soil.'

Thinly and lightly would usually strike the AG as danger-ously nebulous. She is poised to ask how thinly and how lightly when she remembers that the seeds were free, that cornflowers are annuals.

With the scattering of seeds over the surface of the tub, the envy, which she had no idea she harboured, dissipates. She now belongs to the elite. She is a grower from seed. No longer a consumer of takeaways, she is at last, a natural, one hundred per cent organic, home-baker of a gardener.

The anxious gardener
has a stab at spring pruning

The AG is slightly embarrassed to admit that she enjoys pruning. It's licensed aggression. Wandering out into the gar-den, secateurs at the ready, she remembers how her son refused to allow her to cut his nails the minute he was old enough to hold the scissors.

Her first victims are three hardy fuchsias. *Fuchsia magellanica* 'Versicolor', 'Eva Boerg' and 'Mme Cornelissen'. All three are old friends who forgive her her trespasses season after season. She can hack them back right to the stumps and still they resurrect. '*Reculer pour mieux sauter*,' she says aloud as she snips their waving wands.

The lavender bush is another matter. She knows the instructions by heart: 'Cut sparingly with shears but never cut into old wood.' But what if she does cut into dead wood?

'Don't beat about the bush,' says the GM sniggering. 'Chop it. If you do cut into old wood, you just won't get any flowers this year. But leave it and you'll be living with a gaunt, grey-legged monster. And lavenders are a bit like pets, they don't last forever, you have to replace them. Although, at the end of the day, I'm not sure you should replace those

*Eager for more pruning, the Anxious Gardener
sheers the lavender into neat mohicans*

cats of yours. I saw a buddleia the other day that hadn't been spring pruned for three years – a shocking mess.'

The AG sheers the lavender into a neat mohican. Eager for more pruning and loathe to begin the tedious task of sweeping up the snippings, the AG advances on her ceanothus.

'Stop!' cries the GM. 'I thought you said you knew the rules! Only spring prune shrubs that flower after midsummer on this year's growth. Leave all those that flower earlier on the sideshoots of last year's growth.'

The AG stares at the ceanothus which is hurling itself away from the trellis, threatening to bring it down. She longs to prune it back. She hungers for a level garden, a smooth, uniform garden.

'I know how you feel, it's a bit like squeezing a spot instead of waiting for it to resolve in its own time. But believe me, prune the ceanothus now and that's it – no gorgeous blue flowers. *Ceanothus* 'Puget Blue' is my absolute favourite. And when the time comes to prune, take care only to prune back to a live bud. The number of ceanothus I have seen murdered by people who hack back beyond green buds, you wouldn't believe. Although to be fair, ceanothus are known to die young.'

The AG turns her attention to other shrubs that flower on this year's wood. She cuts away the browned top of the spirea 'Anthony Waterer', and ruthlessly removes the green growth of a hypericum. It takes courage to cut back the shrubs she knows to be less hardy, like the blue-flowered *Cerotostigma* and the *Caryopteris*, but they too fall beneath her secateurs.

Sweeping up the snippings, she wonders at her pleasure in order and control.

The anxious gardener
searches for a solution to snails

More and more of the Anxious Gardener's plants are succumbing to slugs and snails. Some suffocate slowly beneath a coat of silver slime, others disappear overnight, still others are reduced to chewed stumps or gnawed stalks. Plant losses usually arouse guilt; snail depredation simply leaves her persecuted. She feels a victim of a hideous injustice. 'All that love and labour, all of that cash poured into the garden centre, simply to provide slug and snail fodder,' she wails.

'Accept limitation,' sagely counsels the Gardening Mentor. 'Plant stuff snails don't fancy. Stick to geraniums. Go cold turkey on dahlias. Work with nature, not against her.'

'I won't give up on asters,' replies the AG. 'There must be a solution. It's so unfair.'

'Squash 'em,' comes the short answer. But the AG is repelled by the noise of cracking shells and the feel of a slippery, rubbery body underfoot.

'Pour salt on them,' advises Maud-Next-Door. But their slow, slimy death is horrible to contemplate.

'No, you just can't use slug pellets,' declares the GM. 'Slug eats pellet, bird eats slug and it's Bye Bye Blackbird. The massive snail overproduction is due to the fact that birds are dying out. You've probably never given much thought to the colour of slug pellets but as a gardener you can't afford not to be curious. The blue pellets contain pheromones which attract slugs and poison them. So when you scatter the granules around a plant you are actually drawing slugs towards that plant. Leave an inch unscattered and they'll be in there munching away.'

The AG confides her snail problem to friends who all promote their personal snail disposal methods. Snail suffering is rife in London.

Snails start falling out of the sky

'Sprinkle bran around the plant.'

'Spread broken eggshells on the flower bed.'

'Freshly ground coffee is a pleasant-smelling deterrent.'

'Copper plant labels do it.'

'Smear Vaseline around a plant pot.'

'Sink a glass of beer in the soil and next day you'll have a pint of drowned slugs and snails.'

'Nothing beats Growing Success – white pellets containing aluminium sulphate.'

'Grapefruit peel, deposited after breakfast.'

The AG fears that her garden will resemble a refuse tip awash with coffee grounds and eggshell, bran, etc. The prospect is so unappealing that she turns to the mail order catalogue in the hopes of discovering aesthetically pleasing snail deterrents. She finds a bright green plastic protective collar which resembles a baby's potty, a black mat to surround the endangered species, rolls of aluminium tape to encase flowerpots. She sends for the lot.

'Waste of money,' sniffs Maud-Next-Door. 'Personally, I hurl them. Project them over the fence. Not, of course into your garden.'

'But what if you're discovered?' exclaims the AG. 'What if snails start falling out of the sky from the direction of your garden? You can't predict the impact of a projected snail.'

'I've thought of that. I'll simply say that I intended to hurl them against the wall and sadly misfired. They're not to know that I was a fast bowler for England's ladies.'

'I've heard that hurled snails head home again.'

'In the interests of science I'll tippex them with a white dot before they go.'

The AG decides that the only solution is mass evacuation. She dons surgical gloves, finds a polythene bag and carries out a thorough sweep of the garden. She lifts overhanging foliage, scrutinises stone edgings and searches the dark side of flowerpots. She collects a satisfying haul. Then she takes the polythene bag and its slimy contents into the street. Surreptitiously she deposits a dozen slugs and snails around the roots of a street tree. It may be labour-intensive but its pro-bird and guilt-free.

'God, Mum, you're really, really sad. You're getting to be like those old persons who feed pigeons. Gross!' exclaims her son, encountering her during an illicit snail drop.

The anxious gardener
confronts repetition compulsion

'Your problem,' says Maud-Next-Door, surveying the AG's beds, 'is that you can't cope with difference.'

'I'm not with you,' replies the AG, all faux-geniality.

'Oh, don't get me wrong,' continues her neighbour, uncharacteristically sweetening the pill, 'I've nothing against mauve. Some say it's insipid, I use the word subtle. But then I have a soft spot for violet cream chocolates. You know, the ones topped by a crystallized violet. I've been known to excavate prematurely a layer in search of a violet cream.'

The mention of violets distresses the AG, reminding her of the recent mass cull of violets, and she is tempted to argue in defence of hard centres, but Maud withdraws. The AG listens to her back door bang and casts a dispassionate eye over her garden. Maud is right. Mauve sits cheek by jowl, or rather petal by leaf, with mauve. Mauve is everywhere; mauve violas, mauve geranium, mauve hebe, mauve nemesia, mauve nameless trumpet-flowered ground cover.

'Do you think there's a slightly pathological tinge to my planting scheme?' she asks the Gardening Mentor.

'Pathological tint? You mean all the mauve. I thought you were doing a Vita Sackville-West.'

'What do you mean?'

A pathological tint to the planting scheme

'That you had in mind her White Garden in mauve, or maybe the Hidcote Red Border in mauve. The Red Border at Hidcote is the only environment that excuses the 'Bishop of Llandaff'. That's one dahlia I can't abide. My mother says that, in her young days, the Bishop was scented. Today the plant gives off not a whiff. Maybe it was considered not appropriate. Maybe it was bred out . . .'

The AG tunes out. Maybe, like her, Vita Sackville-West had accidentally, endlessly raised or purchased white flowers, but making a virtue of repetition compulsion, had declared her garden intentionally monochrome. But the AG feels insufficiently grandiose to declare hers a Mauve Garden. And then there's the unfortunate association to violet cream chocolates.

Mentally the AG retraces the horticultural steps that had led her to match but not mix. In part she blames her inability to think of more than one thing at a time. Searching for simultaneous bloomers, she had purchased the mauve geranium, the mauve campanula and the mauve viola. She had been preoccupied with when they flowered not what they were coloured. And she tends to believe what she sees. The illustrated labels had looked blue or dusty pink.

Her friend Selena, who hitches up with one narcissistic bully after another, comes inexorably to mind. At the start of each relationship, she assures the AG that this time it's different. 'He's really loving,' she says. Three months down the line, he's showing his true colours, as do the AG's plants. Maud is wrong, she thinks, its not that I don't do difference. It's the iron grip of repetition compulsion.

The anxious gardener
listens for applause

The Anxious Gardener understands the desire that fuels the National Garden Scheme, which sells the yellow book giving times and locations of the gardens open to the public, which takes the money on the door, which provides the tea and biscuits. Gardeners may say they want to share the pleasures of their plot, exchanging tips and selling cuttings. But really they long for applause. They long to display their displays. The AG is no different. Her relationship with her garden is mediated through the eyes of others. She anticipates praise and criticism in almost equal measure. But being an anxious gardener, she has a steel-trap recall for garden insults.

There was her friend Alice. They had sat in the garden drinking elderflower cordial on a summer's day when the AG secretly thought her garden looked its best.

'So clever of you to restrict yourself to small-flowered specimens in a small garden,' said Alice, just before catching sight of the bulky lace cap hydrangea poised on the point of flowering. The AG started to make excuses for the hydrangea, citing its capacity for flowering in the shade, for coping with adverse conditions. But the damage was done. It seemed suddenly to the AG that 'Blue Wave' was bulging pinkly out across the garden, rather than, as she had imagined, enlivening a dank corner. Now, whenever she looks at the hydrangea with its generous green leaves, she hears Alice's silent condemnation: 'Far too big for a small garden.' What's more, her mother's voice amplifies Alice's. 'Hydrangeas are so suburban,' she sighs when she catches sight of the lace cap. The AG wonders whether her mother's casual dishing out of horticultural insult is provoked by the religious nature of gardening which breeds intolerance, or by the fashionable approach to gardening which turns a

'Hydrangeas are so suburban,' she sighs

hydrangea into a faux pas. One way or another she swallows the insult on behalf of her shrub.

Sometimes she suspects that envy drives the insults her garden suffers. She certainly thought that was the case with Maud-Next-Door, who popped round to borrow some milk when the garden was truly a peak experience. Maud had hardly glanced at the roses, clematis, geraniums, salvias and anchusas. Instead she had dropped to her knees beside a *Dicentra formosa*, undoubtedly on its last legs. The unfortunate plant was being harried from all sides; by a *Cerastostigma willmottianum* with its speechless periwinkle blue flowers; by a pale blue-mauve clematis called 'Prince Charles' and by a *Geranium psilostemon*. The AG had recently given up the fight on behalf of the dicentra. She had decided to let it be smothered, relying on its amazing capacity to regenerate each year. Maud had leant close to it, exclaiming over it, asking its name, and keeping her back to the delights of the rest of the flower bed. The AG also recalls the friend who caught sight of the rose called 'Yesterday'. It has tiny, dark pink rosette-shaped flowers. The catalogue had described it as mauve. The AG has learned to live with its rosy pink colour, although it dashed her colour scheme.

'What's that?' asked the visitor.

'That's a rose called 'Yesterday'. It's a modern rose with amazing continuity of flowering and disease resistance. Quite a star really.' She had paused, waiting for her friend to praise 'Yesterday'. Total silence ensued. The AG at once regarded 'Yesterday' in a new light. Perhaps it was a little fussy, maybe the colour was a little harsh. Did it clash too grossly with the nearby geranium?

The anxious gardener
is haunted by failures

The Anxious Gardener's garden is awash with ghosts. She is haunted by vanished plants. Shame suffuses her when she allows herself to calculate the cost of the losses. She's talking hard cash here, not hard feelings. But she misses some of the plants, particularly those that lasted long enough for her to become attached to them. She thinks fondly of the variegated *Trachelospermum jasminoides* that put forth white flowers and flourished for a whole year before succumbing to something. She reflects on the different species of horticultural bereavement. First there are the bulbs that never break the surface. Four times she planted *Gladiolus byzantinus* eagerly anticipating the arching stems bearing purple-red flowers. Four times they disappeared without trace. Where bulbs are concerned she suffers not guilt but frustration. 'Hardy, vigorous, elegant and easy,' boasted the bulb's packaging.

'Why?' she asks the Gardening Mentor. 'Why do they let me down time and time again? Why does the womb I prepare so carefully – right depth, right drainage, right aspect – become a tomb?'

'As a gardener you have to learn to take the inexplicable in your stride and look forward to better things next year.'

'Could you perhaps speculate on the fate of the *Gladiolus byzantinus*?' sighs the AG.

'I'd put my money on grave robbers,' replies the GM, 'with squirrels as prime suspects. Although mice are a possibility or even rats.'

'Oh, please!' Nevertheless she's comforted. She is the blameless victim of rampaging rodents. Plants that fail are a different matter. Particularly humiliating is when a plant, known to be easy, vanishes. The shady areas of her garden are haunted by the arching stems and white bells of countless

*She knows she should resign herself to the foothills of
gardening and be grateful for invasive campanula*

failed attempts to establish Solomon's seal. Everyone else's dappled shade is alive with Solomon's seal; hers can't contain them. They hang their heads and expire.

'Where have I gone wrong?' she cries to the GM.

'Insufficiently well drained soil. But personally I don't care for them. You're better off without them. Try *Dicentra spectabilis* – same shape, nice shade of pink and generally more easy going.'

The AG is reminded of the times she tried to plant the children in a summer camp. Other people's children loved them, came home filthy, triumphant and talking of woodlings, trackers and trail seekers, but hers never took root.

When simple, uncomplaining souls like Solomon's seal fail to thrive, the AG feels guilty, but there's a whole group of plants that make her feel out of their league – just not good enough for them. She thinks of meconopsis, the Himalayan poppy, of the tree peony, of agapanthus, alstroemeria and *Nerine bowdenii*. She's tried and failed with all of them. She knows she should resign herself to the foothills of gardening and be grateful for invasive blue campanula rather than raising her eyes to the caerulean heights of meconopsis. But she decides to give the plant one last chance.

Eyeing the bare patch where yet another meconopsis has bitten the dust, Maud-Next-Door sympathises. 'I do know how you feel. It reminds me of when I was a teenager. I knew the best I could hope for was Ringo Starr when I really wanted Paul McCartney.'

The AG feels the comparison is far from apt. The losses she has sustained bring to mind deceased Beatles, Lennon and Harrison, not the living McCartney and Starr.

'Don't beat yourself up,' says the GM. 'They are all tender. Don't take it personally. It's a combination of genetics and environment – and your garden is a harsh one.'

'Don't try and sugar the pill. I know it's a combination of nature and nurture. I'm not a good enough mother.'

The anxious gardener
hesitates to cut back

There's an aquilegia in her garden that affords the AG partic-
ular pleasure. It's a tall plant, stately but tough. It never flops,
flowering well before drought afflicts the garden. Unlike
modern multi-coloured aquilegias, it's all one shade of a
muted, useful red that goes with everything. Though double,
there's nothing vulgar about the flower. The AG usually finds
double flowers faintly embarrassing, 'too-try-hard' as her
children describe unpopular peers. But the aquilegia's flowers
are more fluffy than showy. Best of all it never disappears.
Other plants die down and give the AG a winter of distress,
waiting to see if they survive. Not the aquilegia. It holds onto
its leaves throughout the year.

'Cut it back at the right time, and provided you pick your
moment, it will reward you with a second showing of flowers,' remarks the Gardening Mentor when the Anxious
Gardener sings the praises of the plant.

The AG, longing for a second flush of flowers, nevertheless
procrastinates. She fears that premature decapitation might
simply put paid to the plant rather than provoking more
blooms. Should she wait until the petals fall, leaving bright
green seed pods? Or will the plant be then too old and tired to
manufacture a second flush? She thinks of sticking plasters.
Rip them off too soon and the wound re-opens. Leave them in
place for too long and the skin whitens and wrinkles.

'Does it sound ready to you?' she asks the GM, feverishly
gripping her mobile phone as she peers into the plant. 'Some
petals have shrivelled and the leaves look a little tired.'

'There's no cast-iron answer. You get a feeling when the
time is ripe to cut back. You just know. Trust your intuition.'

The AG knows that the anxious never know. The anxious
watch clocks, take pulses, test the water. To the anxious,

Secateurs gaping, she approaches the
aquilegia. But how far back is back?

intuition is nothing but a snare and a delusion. Nevertheless, secateurs gaping, she approaches the aquilegia. She stops. Cutting back sounds so clean but how far back is back? Should she decapitate the plant or cut it off at the knees? Should leaves be left or the whole plant razed to the ground?

'Be brutal, cut it right back,' decrees the GM. 'Shock it into further production. Actually, leave the healthy leaves.'

Setting about the plant, the AG snips away until nothing is left but a circle of bright, healthy foliage. It's only when she is half way through the French windows that she turns and looks back at the bed. She is reminded of the moment when her children lost their baby teeth. Just as the beautiful symmetry of their mouths was lost, the same has happened with the garden. The disappearance of the aquilegia has wrecked the profile of the border. Her greed has made for a gaping hole. She should have left the plant to die down quietly in its own time.

'Think reincarnation,' says the Gardening Mentor.

The anxious gardener
confronts unpredictability

At times the Anxious Gardener wishes she were a painter and able to apply colour and shape to a space, knowing they would stay in place. She plans the most wonderful combinations of shape and tone in her garden only to have her scheme overturned by natural unpredictability.

She had purchased three verbascums the previous year, intending them to be towering punctuation marks. All were tall, two were dusty pink and one was purple-puce. The latter she positioned alongside a pink sidalcea. Roughly the same height, they made a dramatic couple. Fortunately, all the verbascums survived the winter, throwing up healthy rosettes of

The latest subversion of her best-laid border plans, when the
purple-puce verbascum remained tiny and knee-high to the sidalcea

hardy leaves. But the purple-puce verbascum remained tiny; knee high to the sidalcea which smothered it and soon hid it from view altogether.

Retrieving the verbascum from the unwanted embrace of the sidalcea, the AG reflected that there was a lot to be said for mini-verbascums; they remained upright long after the full-sized plants capsized. But it wasn't what she had planned. The verbascum had been positioned to partner the sidalcea. Had she been conned by the original grower of the plant? Had it been fed some growth-inducing hormone? Or had she inadvertently shrunk it? Guilt and paranoia did battle for her soul.

'I used to feel the same about the children,' sighs Maud-Next-Door, when the AG recounts the verbascum fiasco. 'I just knew that some mother somewhere was providing her children with precisely the right input while I stunted mine.'

'Instead of brooding on accidental failures, focus on inadvertent successes,' counsels the Gardening Mentor. 'Take those two white valerians that you planted in that dark corner. To reach the light, they've grown almost three times their natural size and look terrific poking through the branches of that puce rose 'Marjorie Fair'. Although I have to say, I have never liked 'Marjorie Fair'. She looks like a hydrangea in the throws of a heart attack.'

The GM's swipe at 'Marjorie Fair' reminds the AG of another disappointing incident of inequality in the garden. She had planted two roses: 'Louis XIV', a very dark red China rose advertised as growing to two feet by two feet, and 'Cramoisi Superior', a bright red China rose, advertised as reaching three feet by two feet. She had planted the bright rose behind the dark, imagining Cramoisi peering over the head of Louis XIV. But the latter had rapidly outgrown Cramoisi, completely spoiling her design.

'Be patient,' says the GM, 'Cramoisi may be a late developer. You could try a little cosmetic surgery on Louis XIV or you could add a few inches to Cramoisi by putting it in a pot.'

The AG is not comforted. A pot in the midst of the flower bed seems like cheating to her. She wants her hand to be firmly on the horticultural tiller; happy accidents and 'high heels' won't do. Not only is size unpredictable but her garden has recently suffered from bad timing. She had planted two viticella clematis, intending them to twine together in a companionable yet complementary fashion. At first all went well. The mauve 'Prince Charles' and the purple 'Polish Spirit' mingled enthusiastically. But then at spring pruning time, she cut back Polish Spirit more drastically than Prince Charles. As a result the Prince came and went before Polish Spirit opened even one flower. Polish Spirit was also intended to scramble over and crown a nearby pale pink mallow. But the planned synchronised climbing had been subverted by the degree of shade in her garden. The mallow lagged behind Polish Spirit, its flowering delayed by shade. Their relationship was one-sided to say the least.

'Be a little less Bridget Riley and a bit more Jackson Pollock,' says the Gardening Mentor, when she describes the latest subversion of her best-laid border plans.

The anxious gardener
fears the void

The Anxious Gardener is allergic to bare soil. She wants a fully clothed garden, a garden where earth does its job unseen, where flowers run seamlessly into one another. The words 'ground cover' warm her heart. But even ground cover warningly labelled 'invasive' stands still and refuses to spread in her garden.

*Left to its own devices, the clematis sets off
eagerly in search of new sources of support*

An assiduous reader of garden columns, she comes upon a solution. Clematis that scramble, rather than climb, will twist and weave around shrubs and flowers, blotting out the earth. She imagines the clematis creating a wonderful connective tissue, threading colour through the border.

She purchases a *Clematis* × *durandii* which promises plentiful dark blue flowers. The planting instructions seem somewhat draconian. The deep planting hole must be filled with plenty of organic matter for the plant is a 'gross feeder'. The earth must reach above the bottom buds, which will throw up stems. Its head must be in the sun, its feet in cool shade. She obeys instructions to the letter, planting it in the shade of a small white rose called 'Kent', which she hopes will provide a source of support. She imagines the white rose and the blue clematis mingling in a complementary fashion.

All goes well at first. She feels quite blessed by the clematis. It flowers, it hides the ground, she brings it together with Kent and it threads the rose in a neat and respectful way. She relaxes her vigil and turns her attention elsewhere in the garden. Left to its own devices, the clematis sets off eagerly in search of new sources of support. It hurls itself on top of an emerging scabious, it grabs the young, weak stems of a 'Yesterday' rose and strangles a campanula. The AG hopelessly attempts to disentangle it from its prey. It resists, threatening to snap not only its own stems but those of its new-found host. The AG turns against the clematis. The plant that had once spelled connection and visual coherence is nothing but a boundary breaker.

She considers destroying the plant but it's so strong and healthy. Whereas climbing clematis are light and delicate beings, *C.* × *durandii* is built for a life of scrambling and strangling with leathery, resilient leaves and stiff petals.

'Where did I go wrong?' she asks the Gardening Mentor.

'The clematis was a good idea in the wrong place. Put it in a shrub border and it'll do the business. Put it in a flower bed and it will flatten all before it.'

'What if I cut it back and watch it like a hawk?'

'It's up to you really. I know what I would do.'

The AG decides to keep the clematis under constant supervision for one last summer.

The anxious gardener
turns to natural born killers

The Anxious Gardener tells herself her garden is too small for the dose of insecticide she's applying to upset the environment. To be honest, she is more concerned for her own health than the eco-state of the world. Hypochondria is a greater motivator than ecological concern. Fear is more powerful than shame. Her fear of the impact of insecticides on her own, her children's and her cats' health outweighs her anxiety in relation to their environmental impact. Yet even fear can be overridden. The sight of the children and the cats scratching, and the soft, hopeful tips of the roses encrusted with aphids again and again sends her running for bug killer.

Until the day of the simultaneous infestation. Arriving home from work, the AG turns to glance at 'Souvenir du Docteur Jamain' snaking up beside the front door. Even though it is early spring, the doctor is clotted with aphids. Once upon a time there was a seasonal respite from insects but global warming has led to unremitting infestation. The AG sighs, turns the key in the lock and pushes open the front door only to be confronted by children and cats scratching in unison. A quick comb of hair and fur discloses colonies of nits and fleas. The AG, however, decides to treat the doctor and goes in search of Roseclear.

Donning gloves, a surgical mask, a headscarf and Wellington boots, the AG advances on the rose. Even as the

Souvenir du Docteur Jamain is clotted with aphids

aphids die beneath the spray, she recalls that Roseclear was recently cleared from the shelves for containing a substance noxious to humans, let alone fish and pets. True it had been re-issued with a clean bill of health, but for how long? The direction of the wind suddenly shifts blowing a fine toxic mist into her face. As for Docteur Jamain, no longer being eaten alive, he is nevertheless coated with dead insects.

Even more frightening is the cats' insecticide. The instructions on the packet warn against touching the cat for eight hours after application. How is she to prevent the children stroking the cats or the cats stroking the children? The children's insecticide is reassuringly called a crème rinse. But the AG is not deceived. She knows she is tipping insecticide over her innocent, nit-ridden children's heads. It's then that she decides to go cold turkey on bug-killers.

Another ecologically-sound mother tells her about tea tree oil. The children hate the smell and cry for insecticide, but she discovers a certain, perhaps phylogenetic, pleasure in combing for nits. She deals with the cats' fleas by feeding them a substance that stops the fleas reproducing. That leaves the roses. How is she to combat their parasites?

'If I had a bigger garden with more roses, I'd share them with the aphids,' she says to the Gardening Mentor.

'And if you had more children, you'd share them with the nits?'

'OK, OK, tell me what to do.'

'You could let ladybirds deal with them for you.'

'I'd need a red army of ladybirds to deal with this lot.'

'No problem. There's a mail order catalogue that supplies ladybird breeding kits and a ladybird bag, containing one hundred ladybird larvae to hang in trees. And you can purchase ladybird houses – hibernation homes in which they overwinter.'

The AG has a fondness and sympathy for ladybirds which goes back to childhood and the nursery rhyme about the anxious ladybird flying home to deal with a fire which has decimated her children. She likes the idea of festooning her garden with bags of ladybird larvae and ladybird houses. But the immediate problem of aphids remains.

'Then there's lacewings,' continues the GM. 'The larvae come in bottles of two hundred. Each one kills fifty aphids or greenfly a day, although it makes one wonder who has been counting. They're basically provided for greenhouses but you can apply spot treatments outdoors. Just shake the bottle over the effected areas. I've found mail order delivery of ladybirds and lacewings really reliable. They replace them if they are found dead on arrival.'

'Hardly a now solution,' sighs the AG gazing at 'Madame Alfred Carrière' concealed between the weight of a million aphids.

'The simplest thing is just to squash them, but you'll be too squeamish for that. So all you need to do at this time of the year is just give a quick flick to the stem and off they'll tumble.'

The AG flicks a stem of Mme Carrière. Weakened by infestation it snaps and falls to the ground. The GM looks a little chastened.

'Well, you could wash them off with the jet of the hose.'

'Hosing feels too random.'

'There are increasing numbers of non-toxic sprays on the market. Just Bug Killer, for example, smothers and suffocates. Then there's always Ecover. Dilute some Ecover washing-up liquid, put it in a spray and the fatty acids should do the trick. But then again it might not. At the end of the day, nothing works like a toxic spray.'

Feeling like a smoker tossing their final packet into the fire, the AG tips the contents of an insecticide spray down the drain, inhaling the familiar chemical perfume. Then she fills the bottle with diluted Ecover.

As she douses Mme Carrière with gently frothing Ecover,

she reflects on the profound pleasure of shameless, fear-free spraying. But the aphids seem to shrug off the washing-up liquid, leaving the AG longing for the era when ignorance was bliss, when antibiotics were administered repeatedly and toxins sprayed liberally with impunity.

The anxious gardener
is unhappy with helianthemums

Known as rock roses, they sounded so good on paper. 'Spreading plant which provides a brilliant show of numerous flowers for many weeks from June onwards.' There was a good handful to choose from: 'Wisley Pink', with 'soft pink flowers and silvery grey foliage'; 'Raspberry Ripple', 'as delightful as its name implies'; 'Snow Queen' and 'Ben Hope', with 'lovely rosy flowers'. The AG often wonders about the naming of flowers. Who was Ben Hope? How admirably secure he must be in his gender identity for a small flowered pink plant to bear his name. She will definitely include him amongst her rock roses.

The AG envisages rock roses tumbling in profusion from the raised bed above her patio. People seated in her kitchen, catching sight of the spectrum of pinks cascading towards the patio, will exclaim in wonderment. She'll say, 'Yes, aren't they lovely. Rock roses . . . Ben Hope. Very easy really. Can I give you a little more pasta? Yes, they are evergreen.'

She plants the helianthemum in well-manured soil and intersperses them with a few tough early flowerers, aubretia and small-leaved vinca. But far from providing 'a brilliant show of numerous flowers' the rock roses are withholding. Despite growing at a healthy rate, they produce only the odd, brief, flower. The AG blames the sun. The plants are sundependent and deprived.

Ben Hope is clinging to life

Winter comes and with the first frost the supposed-ever-green leaves fall to the ground. Only the one with dullest green leaves remains intact. Unfamiliar with the habits of helianthemum, the AG decides to wait until spring before despairing. Come spring, however, nothing stirs on the tangled twiggy stems of the helianthemum.

'Sorry to have to tell you,' says the Gardening Mentor, 'but they're all corpses, except for this one.'

Sadly, the AG pulls out the remains of 'Raspberry Ripple', 'Wisley Pink' and 'Snow Queen'. Ben Hope is clinging to life.

'What about Ben Hope, will he spread over and down the wall of the raised bed?'

'You're joking, of course.'

'Unintentionally.'

'To grow down the wall, would be to turn his back on the sun. Plants grow towards the sun.'

Gripped by her fantasy garden, the AG had denied what she knew. Of course, she knew plants grew towards the sun. She frowns at the surviving helianthemum. A few pitiful leaves cling to the very tips of its twisting grey stems.

'What'll I do with it? Euthanasia?'

'To be honest you've treated it all wrong. Helianthemums like harsh conditions, stony ground and strong sun. You've overfed it. You've mollycoddled it.'

The AG recalls her mother on the subject of her children: 'You spoil those children. You make it all too easy for them. I'm amazed they can tie their own shoe laces.' Actually they enter and exit their trainers with laces knotted but she keeps that from her mother.

'Look at that lavender,' continues the GM, pointing at a scraggy lavender leaning across the garden path. 'Same story – too much rich food. Stick to aubretia: dull but reliable.'

The aubretia is, indeed, alive, but somehow the Anxious Gardener can't imagine it eliciting cries of admiration from the kitchen.

The anxious gardener
procrastinates

Every day the Anxious Gardener gazes out of the window at 'Dublin Bay', which is calling for help. The dark red flowering rose is in dire need of dead-heading. Yet the AG does nothing. Her secateurs remain firmly closed.

'Forgive me,' says her friend Mary, seated at the kitchen table in sight of the rose. 'It's none of my business but you're neglecting 'Dublin Bay' and depriving yourself of a second flush in the process.'

The AG is not galvanized. 'Oh, I'm such a procrastinator,' she confesses.

'Procrastination is nothing more than adolescent rebellion,' says Mary. 'You just won't do as you're told.'

But the AG feels as if Mary's intervention on behalf of the rose has exonerated her; as if care of the rose has passed to Mary. 'It won't flower again unless you take action,' warns her friend. The AG knows it and still she procrastinates.

Why, she asks herself, despite her permanent state of anxiety on behalf of her garden, does she practise horticultural procrastination? Possibly procrastination is unconsciously intended to precipitate action, through the building up of intolerable levels of anxiety. Perhaps procrastination satisfies masochism. Certainly the growing pile of snippings and clippings on the patio, waiting to be swept up, causes her constant pain. Maybe procrastination is a way of short-circuiting horticultural perfectionism. She thinks of violas. A television programme had been unequivocal on the importance of shaving violas in September. Her violas are stretching desperately in all directions. Maybe fear of sadism lies behind her inability to shear back the violas. Maybe she's just not certain how far back to cut them.

Then there's the issue of 'Clair Matin'. The pink rose is breaking free of the trellis. It would take her five minutes and

Dublin Bay is calling for help

a search for some twine to secure the rose to its moorings. Unless she takes action, the rose is likely to fall victim to the first high winds of autumn. She does nothing.

Maud-Next-Door takes up the cause of the rose. Pointing to the waving wands, she inquires of the AG's intentions.

'Do you think I'm congenitally lazy?' the AG asks her neighbour.

'No, only Geminis and Librans are fundamentally lazy,' comes the reply. 'I see procrastination as a defence against fear of death. It suggests a permanent tomorrow.'

'I don't agree,' replies the AG. 'To my mind procrastination is dicing with death. Look at that Busy Lizzy in my window box, facing death due to my delayed watering.'

'What I mean,' perseveres Maud, 'is that outstanding gardening tasks fill the void. They're a plea for immortality.'

'No,' answers the AG. 'If anything, procrastination provides petrol for the gardener, finally fuelling action.' And turning from Maud, she hurries at last to the aid of 'Clair Matin'.

SUMMER

The anxious gardener
is overwhelmed by bindweed

Anxiety has an important place in the gardener's toolkit. Anxiety keeps the gardener on her toes and forever on the job. Hence, holidays induce intense separation anxiety in the AG. She rarely leaves home. For her the sight of a dry, sandy beach evokes an image of a parched garden. When forced to leave for foreign climes, she organises plantsitting but the prospect of returning to a bare and desiccated, or choked and overabundant plot takes away the pleasure of travel.

Watching the AG overwatering on the eve of her departure for Greece, Maud-Next-Door is deeply sympathetic: 'I know just how you feel. It reminds me of what I went through when I left the children at nursery. You just never knew what would be waiting for you when you returned to collect. I recall the guilt as if it were yesterday.'

Bindweeed is waiting for the AG when she returns home, drops suitcases on the doorstep and flies through the house to the garden. Dozens of corkscrews of bindweed have taken advantage of her absence to scale and throttle her plants.

'The Times' rose has dropped its beautiful dark red leaves in protest at the parasite wound around its stems. The brilliant flowers of a hardy fuchsia have shrivelled and died for want of light and air, smothered by bindweed. And most poignant of all, bindweed has raced up the stems of a tall aster that the AG had transplanted from a friend's garden shortly after her death. She had, of course, worried that the aster would succumb to mildew but it had flourished. The AG had taken it as a sign from her friend that 'all was forgiven'. Now the poor plant's stalks were bowed to the ground beneath the ruthless assault of countless tendrils of bindweed.

How right she had been to worry. How wrong to have gone on holiday.

Corkscrews of bindweed scale and throttle her plants

How unbearable to be brought face to face with annihilation. 'I don't want to know,' she cries aloud, retreating to the kitchen and burying her face in her hands. She fumbles for the phone.

'Bindweed,' she sobs to the Gardening Mentor.

'I won't pretend it isn't serious. One stem of bindweed can presage the disintegration of the entire garden. Suffocation. Weed killer is the only solution, but wait until everything has died down before you apply it. And wear gloves. I well remember a friend of mine who let bindweed take hold . . .'

Quietly the AG breaks the connection. Far from containing her anxiety, the GM is stoking it. Weedkiller feels somehow like cheating. Only direct and maybe masochistic action will soothe her. After all, she has only herself to blame.

She begins with first aid to the strangled fuchsia. Carefully she pursues a strand of bindweed to earth and pulls. It snaps. She excavates the root only to discover a veritable spaghetti junction of bindweed beneath the surface of the soil. Cure will clearly constitute a serious challenge. Going for a short-term solution she addresses the symptoms and carefully unwinds a corkscrew tendril from a stem of the aster. It is far harder than she expects. The bindweed won't be parted from the aster. Rage, impatience and a sense of persecution get the better of her. Soon she is yanking at the parasite, stripping the leaves of the host and snapping the already weakened stalk.

'Bindweed!' exclaims Maud-Next-Door, peering through the trellis. 'Fearfully clingy, isn't it? Leave even a morsel of root behind and you'll be dealing with the return of the repressed.'

The anxious gardener
steers clear of variegated varieties

It was *Liriope muscari* that set the Anxious Gardener thinking about variegation. A gardening column had alerted her to
the advantages of *Liriope muscari*, extolling the plant's
resilience, tolerance of shade and late flowering period. With
its broad grass-like foliage and many flower spikes of bright
violet mauve, it sounded irresistible. The Anxious Gardener
was nevertheless nonplussed by the plant's name. She had
always thought that muscari was the proper name for grape
hyacinths, those bulbous plants that appear in spring along
with crocuses and chionodoxas. A mail order catalogue
solved the puzzle informing her that, 'the flowers bear a
resemblance to muscari, hence its name'.

The catalogue offered not only *Liriope muscari* but also
Liriope muscari 'Gold-banded' with 'a clear golden band to
the edge of the foliage'. The AG is charmed and orders three
plain and three variegated *Liriope muscari*, even though the
latter were significantly more expensive.

She planted them in equally salubrious spots and treated
them with scrupulous fairness. Unfortunately, her cats developed a taste for them. They indiscriminately ate both the
plain and gold-banded. The plants fought for their lives, and
once the leaves had aged, the cats left them alone. The AG
was reminded of her relief when her children grew too old to
be bullied in the playground. But despite surviving feline
depredation, the variegated variety slowly shrunk and disappeared.

The vanishing of the variegated *Liriope muscari* distresses
the AG. The history of variegation in her garden, she admits
to herself, is a sorry tale of woe. She's always gone for variegated varieties in the belief that should they suffer flower-fail-
ure, a pretty leaf will earn them a place in the border. But all

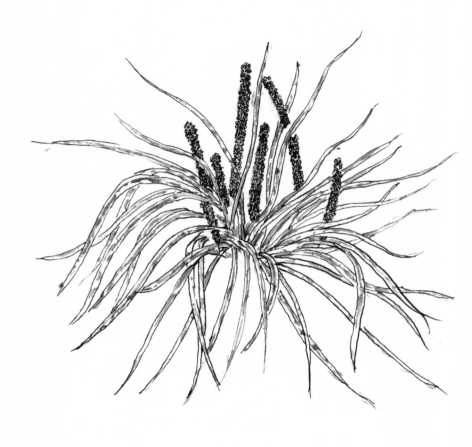

The history of variegated plants in her garden is a tale of woe

her variegated plants have died young. The gloomy roll call includes a variegated trillium (which maybe doesn't count as she has failed to grow even plain trillium), a variegated aubrietia, the brunnera 'Dawson's White' and the erysimium 'Cotswold Gem'. The failure of a variegated pulmonaria and a delightful variegated polemium had astonished her. She had thought both plants indestructible.

'Is it me or are variegated varieties particularly weak and oversensitive?' she asks the Gardening Mentor.

'Think bulldogs and boxers,' comes the reply. 'Compared to your average full-nosed hound, they're the delicate flowers of the canine world. Anything bred for abnormality will be problem-prone. There's nothing natural about a variegated aubretia.'

'What about variegated ivy, lamium or *Fuchsia magellanica* 'Versicolor'?'

'They're the old-hands of the blotched brigade. They've proved themselves. You must resist when you see newly variegated varieties. Anyway, why are you such a sitting duck for variegation? Personally, I would rather have an all black cat than a black and white Jellicle cat.'

The very next day, the AG finds a catalogue lying seductively on the doormat. It falls open at *Sedum alboroseum* 'Mediovariegatum', £4.50 for three.

She gazes at the fluffy pink flowers rising from bright cream-splashed leaves.

Sedums are such useful plants, providing such reliable autumn colour but she has never cared for their blue-green glaucous leaves. Now here is a sedum with a difference. She imagines the multi-coloured leaves lifting and enlivening the late summer bed.

'Think bulldog, think Jellicle cat,' she exclaims aloud.

The anxious gardener
suffers horticultural amnesia

'Can you tell me the name of that shrub over there?' asks Maud-Next-Door, crossing a boundary, peering through the trellis. 'That one, with the blue trumpet-shaped flowers.'

A familiar sensation, the liquefying and draining away of memory, overcomes the Anxious Gardener.

'That one!' cries Maud, failing to get a reply. 'The one in the far corner behind the delphiniums.'

Maud waits expectantly while passivity cloaks the AG. The name resides somewhere in her body, just out of her reach.

'Oh God,' she cries, 'I know it as well as I know my own name.'

'Well?'

'I think it begins with B,' replies the AG, playing for time, 'It's something like bougainvillea.'

'It's certainly not a bougainvillea,' says Maud, sounding a touch triumphant. The mask of the knowing gardener is slipping from the AG and it warms the heart of her neighbour.

'I know all about it,' desperately exclaims the AG, shaking her head as if to kick-start her mind. 'It's a late flowerer. The blue trumpets collapse soon after flowering. We saw loads of them along motorways in the South of France last summer. I think it's got a name like *Campsis* 'Mme Galen', except, of course, that's a climber with orange trumpets.'

Maud becomes sympathetic: 'I do know the problem. I can only remember flowers with proper names to whom I'm properly introduced, like the rose 'Madame Alfred Carrière' or the clematis 'General Sikorsky'. Maybe it's that shrub that became so very popular some years ago. It began with M.'

Maud is torturing the AG. 'Barnsley,' Maud cries. 'The more tasteful pale pink variety was called 'Barnsley'.'

Hibiscus – as ever, once a name is unearthed,
she is left with a sense of anti-climax

'No,' sighs the AG, 'it's not a mallow, though I grant you it looks like one.' At least 'mallow' has not left her mind.

'Well, never mind,' says Maud having done her worst. 'Let me know when it comes to you. It's age, of course – oestrogen deficiency.' She withdraws from the trellis, like a tortoise into her shell, thinks the AG, reflecting sadly that gardening comes with age – and goes with age. Yesterday she pulled a muscle lugging compost – poor recompense for having bought organic and peat-free – and today the name escapes her not only of That Shrub but also of the Tree-in-the-Right-Hand-Corner. It's like forgetting the names of your own children, she thinks, and the blank strikes her as intolerable.

Is this the onset of dementia? Will her borders slowly sink into total anonymity? Will the name of one flower after the other fade from her mind? Frightened she goes in search of *The Reader's Digest: A Garden for All Seasons*. She knows she'll know the name when she sees it. And, indeed, there under 'Shrubs for Autumn', *The Reader's Digest* waxes purple over the hibiscus: 'Hope for a warm, dry summer to enjoy to the full the hibiscus's sumptuous, deep blue-mauve blooms, with their dramatic cone of stamens.'

Hibiscus – as ever, once a name is unearthed, she is left with a sense of anti-climax. She had, after all, known it all along. Then the AG has an idea that deeply reassures. It's not that the muscles of her mind are failing; the mechanics of repression are in fine working order. She simply forgets the names of flowers with awkward associations. Once, when moving house, she had broken the contract and secretly abducted a hibiscus from the old garden and taken it with her to the new. The wages of sin had been the death, almost instantly, of the hibiscus.

Fired, she searches for the lost name of the Tree-in-the-Right-Hand-Corner. Of coure, it is an amelanchier. She had known it was an amelanchier. Every year, *The Reader's Digest* tells her, 'without fail, the hardy and reliable amelanchier gives two fine performances.' In spring it produces 'a breathtaking snowfall of starry white flowers' and in autumn it is 'bedecked in foliage of flaming oranges and reds'.

She knows now why her mind wouldn't speak the name amelanchier. Her ex was forever extolling the gardening taste and competence of his ex in choosing to plant a neat, compact, high-performance amelanchier. Next time when someone asks her to name a flower, silently she'll dig around for the original trauma, locate it and with ease retrieve the repressed name.

The anxious gardener
weeds in ignorance

The beds are beginning to resemble those little boxes of watercress propagated and shorn for salad bowls The Anxious Gardener does her best to persuade herself that the 'watercress' is evidence that something has seeded. She peers hopefully at the little green shoots but doubt creeps in. Could they be weeds? Shame can't be kept at bay. She will be censored, condemned and dubbed a lazy gardener whose neglected plot has 'run to seed'. Her plants will be 'choked'. The weeds will 'take over'. She will be spied desperately, furtively applying weed killer. She remembers the day her homeopath discovered that she dosed her children with Calpol – and shudders.

Breathing deeply, she tells herself to wait, to let the watercress declare itself and show its true colours. It might well be a reproducing resident rather than an outsider involved in a takeover bid. But rather than growing up, the watercress grows sideways, spreading into an impenetrable mat. Her newly planted roses are being denied the earth around them.

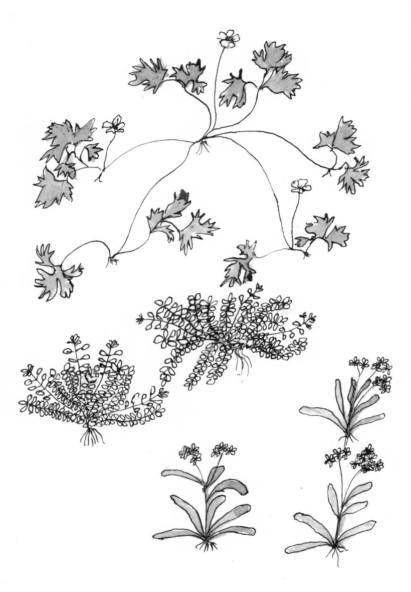

*It might be a reproducing resident rather than
an outsider involved in a takeover bid*

She is now not only ashamed but frightened for her roses. Her children join her in contemplation of the anonymous growth and the left-leaning son accuses her of elitism, of discriminating against weeds.

'It's matter out of place,' she replies, 'in a Mary Douglas kind of way. Cat hairs are all very well on the cat but not on the sofa.' But still she hesitates and still the watercress withholds its identity.

'What's that?' asks Maud-Next-Door peering through the trellis that divides their gardens. That did it. Suffused with shame, the AG goes in search of a handfork. Later in her own defence she likened the moment to being told that she had chocolate round her mouth.

Weeding proves wonderfully satisfying, particularly when she seizes and evicts a known intruder, like groundsel. Pulling it out, roots intact, feels a real achievement. Of course, there are tense moments when she sees she has grubbed up a scabious or pulled at and snapped a root attached to a penstemon. But finally all that remain are known plants, surrounded by clean, pure, lightly forked earth. Shame expunged, the Anxious Gardener gets somewhat stiffly to her feet.

'I'll take those.'

The AG spins round to find the Gardening Mentor rooting through the pile of evicted watercress.

'Forget-me-nots are so useful. They make really great ground cover. Just dig them up when they start to go mildewy and they'll be back in place, doing the job, next year.'

'Forget-me-nots?'

'Well, you've a bit of *Lychnis coronaria* lying here with them but I won't take that. You can keep lychnis, as far as I'm concerned. I know some people really rate the silver leaves and puce flowers, but personally, I find them too dominant. To be honest, I've often wondered about your liking for lychnis. Clearly you've seen the light at last. You haven't left a seedling, have you?'

The anxious gardener
is led into temptation

Summer is a moment of peak temptation for the catalogue addict. They tumble thick and fast onto the Anxious Gardener's doormat where they lie provocatively within their plastic wrappers. They all know her: Parker's, Blom's, Austin's, etc. They have her number. The only way to maintain blank order forms is to bin the lot without opening them. Catalogue addicts are never cured. But, surely, she thinks, she could just leaf through Parker's, simply skim the herbaceous perennials. 'Just looking,' she murmurs as she tears open the wrapping.

She is saved by the bell – the front door bell.

'What is that I see in your hand?' asks the Gardening Mentor. 'Tell me it's not Parker's wholesale.'

The AG looks down, feigning surprise.

'If you really can't resist, go through it while I'm here. Select what you want and I'll weed out the mistakes.'

Gratefully, the AG immerses herself in thumbnail sketches of plants on offer. Words hook the AG. For example, 'cascade' she finds completely irresistible. Parker's provides a description of aubretia that sends her hunting for the order form – 'prolific', 'cascading', 'carpeting'. Ten plants are offered for four pounds.

'But you are already well stocked with aubretia,' exclaims the GM.

'Mine are mauve. I want red aubretia.'

'You lack catalogue canniness. You can buy aubretia in any garden centre. You'll be in control of their time of arrival, their state of health, and their size. Given your anxiety levels, you must limit your consumption from catalogues.'

Fortunately the next words to catch the AG's eye are 'popular' and 'double'. Elitist that she is, nothing would induce

She will live with the permanent regret of having
parsimoniously passed up Queen of the Night

her to order Mrs Bradshaw 'the popular double red geum'. But closing the catalogue she spies the word 'robust'. Achilleas, she reads, are 'robust, colourful and easy'. In other words irresistible.

'Only the other day you compared achillea unfavourably to Queen Anne's lace.'

Next the AG falls for a 'resilient' *Gaillardia*. The GM reminds her that she hates yellow. Then the word 'easy' jumps off the page. How can she possibly pass up a plant categorised as 'easy'? She reads aloud:

'*Papaver* 'Turkenlouis' is easy to grow and very attractive. The new hairy foliage in spring is very pleasing. It bears fascinating shaped red flowers with dark centres.'

'Are you seriously going to take the word of someone who finds new hairy growth pleasing? Are you actually basing your purchase on the opinion of that person?'

Regretfully the AG abandons the prospect of a fascinating poppy, only to catch sight of a monarda described as 'useful'.

'Does it say what it's useful for, beyond introducing mildew into the borders? Your approach to catalogues is fundamentally too passive. Supposing you see a flower at Chelsea that you like? Remember how you fell in love with sweet rocket last year? That would have been a moment to use a catalogue. You knew what you wanted and why. Although, personally, I wouldn't touch sweet rocket. It seeds about far too freely for my liking.'

'OK, point taken. I know I am catalogue-gullible. But I have been thinking about hellebores ever since spring. I've put a lot of thought into hellebores. I have been considering their colour, their size, their time of flowering and their ideal environment. I'd like to fill that dark, eastern corner of the garden with hellebores and Parker's have a number of different colours.'

What the AG doesn't say is that one of the hellebores on offer is described as 'nearly black' – words that invariably hook her. 'Queen of the Night'; surely, she thinks, the GM can have no objections to 'Queen of the Night'. It wouldn't be a spontaneous purchase; she has been planning on hellebores. The only slight problem is that the catalogue is selling them at twenty pounds for ten. Can she really accommodate ten 'nearly black' hellebores in her small garden? But what if she fails to take advantage of the offer? The plant may never again cross her path. She will live with the permanent regret of having parsimoniously and cautiously passed up 'Queen of the Night'. And surely ten hellebores for twenty pounds is an umissable bargain?

'Think internet dating,' the GM interrupts her thoughts. 'Do you do it? No you don't. I rest my case. But I must leave you. Before I go, I suggest we bin the catalogues together.'

The seeds of desire have been sown. Hardly has the door closed on the Gardening Mentor when the Anxious Gardener rushes to the computer. Someone, she can't remember who, has told her of a wonderful site for purchasing plants online.

The anxious gardener
hungers for originality

A child of the radical seventies, the Anxious Gardener has set her face against the idealisation of originality. No artist works in isolation, she's wont to say. All works of art are the product of a network of influences. Genius is a man-made concept. And she truly believes it. Which makes her deeply ashamed of her reaction, in her friends Mary's garden, on first catching sight of the geranium 'Ann Folkard' weaving its magenta way through the bright blue flowers of a *Ceratostigma willmotianum.*

'Plagiarist!' she wants to shout. 'My idea!'

To be strictly honest the combination was a happy accident. Although she had heard Ann Folkard described as a bully she

The geranium 'Ann Folkard' weaving its magenta way through the blue flowers of Ceratostigma willmotianum

had never expected her to turn into a climber, scrambling all over the *Ceratostigma willmotianum*. She well remembers showing Mary the combination in her garden, omitting the accidental aspect of it. Secretly, she'd had her doubts. The plumbago and the geranium didn't quite match but Mary had reassured her that their voices mingled successfully. Her friend's cries of admiration had, indeed, been music to her ears. Ripped off, she says to herself, eyeing the geranium/ plumbago mix. 'Wonderful combination,' she says aloud to Mary, hoping for an acknowledgment or at least a footnote.

'Mmm,' murmurs her friend.

On leaving Mary's, urgently she phones the Gardening Mentor.

'When does inspiration become plagiarism? Is it shameful to want copyright?' she wails into her mobile, hoping she won't be treated to that unsatisfying platitude – imitation is the highest form of flattery.

'Remember the song we sang as children "Copy cat, dirty rat, stick your head in bacon fat"? How would you feel if you showed up at a party in the same dress as the hostess?'

The AG imagines the laughter, the explanations, the secret appraisal of which woman looked best in the garment.

'And what shape were her plants in? Healthier than yours?'

'I think I'll go now.'

She closes the mobile and reflects on the curious cultural place of the garden. It's classified as craft not art, copyright law doesn't apply to flower arrangements, and yet horticultural competition flourishes and horticultural envy is rampant. Would it be poaching, she wonders, to adopt Mary's placement of a *Lychnis coronaria* cheek by jowl with a nepeta? It did work exceedingly well. The silver leaves of the *Lychnis coronaria* and its generous small magenta flowers agreed so well with the pale blue mauve, airy nepeta. No one would know it wasn't her idea. Should she ask permission? Would Mary notice?

The anxious gardener
copes with the collapse of a sidalcea

No warning signs prepared the Anxious Gardener for the collapse; not even the hint of a droop, a curl of a leaf or bending of a stem. She emerges for her morning inspection of the garden to find the sidalcea seemingly in a dead faint. No longer reaching for the sky with its spires of dusty pink flowers, it lies horizontal to the ground in a rosette of misery. Rage and self-reproach do battle for the AG's soul. What has she done? Why has the sidalcea done this to her?

'I'm afraid it is your fault,' says the Gardening Mentor over the phone. 'You really only have yourself to blame. You let it dry out, didn't you? The Consumers Association said two out of three plants (or is it one out of three?) die just due to drought.'

'But the man at the garden centre said it loved full sun.'

'In moisture retentive soil! Read the small print.'

'So what do I do? Will it get to its feet with a good soaking?'

'I doubt it. It's too tall to recover its poise. Give it a good soaking and then prune it back to little buds. To be honest, you should have had a support system already in place. Sidalceas tend to collapse without warning.'

Replacing the receiver, the AG berates herself. Why is she so bad at forward planning? Why did she not have prosthetic sticks at the ready for the poor sidalcea? Her garden should be studded with carefully concealed sources of support. But besieged by immediate worries she is always unwilling to look ahead at what the future holds for her flowers. Turning her back on the scene of her crime, she goes in search of bamboos. But like umbrellas, gloves and sunglasses, they have a tendency to vanish. The house is bare of bamboos. The AG brightens. The lack provides an excuse to visit the garden centre.

Entering the garden centre she is at once enticed by fox-

The sidalcea lies horizontal to the ground in a rosette of misery

gloves. Shade loving, they would go beautifully in the end of the garden beneath the trees. Perhaps she should buy just one foxglove and see how it manages. One foxglove is tantamount to buying a two-fingered Kit Kat. She selects four foxgloves. Their leathery leaves and chunky stems, will surely survive hard times without swooning.

'You bought four foxgloves!' exclaims the GM later. 'I have to tell you that in London I've never bought a foxglove that worked. Even those with leathery leaves disappear without flowering. I've thought to myself, well all right, they're biennials, maybe I'll see them next year. But I never see them again. What does work is scattering seeds. Here's what I'd do: keep them in a pot on the patio, preserve the heads and scatter the seeds.'

The garden centre offers a range of staking solutions; including a rather appealing contraption of green metal hoops and stakes which can be combined and arranged to forestall any collapse. A glance at the price tag sends the AG hurrying for the bamboos. All the middle-sized bamboos have already been purchased. Plants must be falling down all over London. The AG is vaguely comforted to be one of a crowd. She hesitates between the giant and pygmy canes. She imagines trying to break a big bamboo: the splintering, the splitting. She opts for the short.

'I have to say, bamboos are a mixed blessing,' says the GM. 'Did they come with a green cap? No? Well, for heaven's sake, take care. Eyes, eyes, eyes. Bend over and they'll stab you in the eye. What's more, bamboos can rot. And then if you use bamboos over and over again, they begin to harbour pests and diseases.'

The AG explains that bamboos in her possession quickly go AWOL, hence things lurking in the depths of old bamboos is one worry less.

'That makes a change,' says the GM somewhat snidely. 'Although speaking of staking, Monty Don has a really nice idea. He uses copper poles, bits of old plumbing. Copper is becoming really popular as a way of keeping slugs and snails off. So the stake would kill two birds with one stone. He also uses stair rods, but to my mind they are a bit sharp and small. The great thing about metal, even though copper pipe isn't cheap, is that it doesn't rot and it blends in when it goes green or rusty.'

The AG will never seek out or re-use copper pipe, however slug proofing it might be. Garden as scrap metal yard holds no appeal. She will stick with bamboos.

'In that case,' says the GM, 'try staking naturally. Collect switches of willow, birch, chestnut or whatever, before they come into bud. Dry them out, shove them in the ground around the plant, a little shorter than the plant's final destination, and when the plant falls, the twigs will catch them. They'll be hidden from view before you know it.'

As far as the AG goes, out of sight is not out mind. A garden strewn with dried sticks is almost as unappetizing as a garden of scrap mettle. She decides to stick with bamboos.

'But they're dead wood!' exclaims the GM.

Advancing on the horizontal sidalcea, she wonders how many bamboos it needs to stay upright. The prospect of a border bristling with bamboos is almost as bad as old piping. She decides on two, one on either side of the plant. The state of the soil confirms the Gardening Mentor's diagnosis. Packed hard and dry, it resists the bamboo cane. However forcibly she pushes the cane, the earth refuses to accept it. She shifts the cane a little to one side, hoping to find the earth's weak spot. But still it won't accommodate the bamboo. She leans on the bamboo with all her weight. It snaps. She falls. Eyes, she thinks, and screws them shut. A stem of sidalcea crushes beneath her.

At last she has two bamboos in place – though shakily. Kneeling, string in hand, she fondly embraces the fallen plant, gathering it into an upright position. A couple of stalks evade capture. She releases the rest of the plant, disentangling string and leaves. Once more she imprisons the plant in a charmed circle of string but then accidentally loses one end of the string, and as she fumbles for it, the plant again sinks to the earth. Hatred for the sidalcea swamps concern. Brutally she tightens string around stalk, knots it, stands back and sighs. The sidalcea appears garrotted. Like a corseted woman, it will grow sick and deformed. She loosens the string. A few stalks slip the collar. By now quite hostile to the sidalcea, the AG leaves them to their fate. It's then that the AG understands that crooked stems are the wages of being slow to stake. The sidalcea, having grown accustomed to life lived at the horizontal, has lifted its head to the sun. Now, though vertical, each stem has a crick in its neck. Hot, cross and discouraged the AG abandons the garden.

Next day the AG trails glumly into the garden to check on the patient, only to find herself forgiven. The plant has straightened, pointing skywards once more. And, in a conciliatory fashion, it has bushed out, concealing its belt of string.

The anxious gardener
abandons hope

Like recalling a holiday romance, the Anxious Gardener fondly remembers the summer that three anchusas flourished and flowered for her. The tall plants had produced their electric blue flowers from June to August just as the catalogue had promised. They had seemed entirely hardy, at ease in the AG's soil and perfectly happy to do without full sun. But the following Summer the AG had scrutinized the soil in vain. The anchusas had abandoned her.

'Never say die!' said the Gardening Mentor, with irritatingly joviality. 'Easy come, easy go, and they are indeed easy, so buy some more.'

However, her first attempt to re-establish anchusa had led

*Like recalling a holiday romance, the Anxious Gardener remembers
the summer that three anchusas flourished and flowered for her*

to an ineradicable attack of eryngium. By mistake the mail order company had dispatched blue thistles instead of blue anchusa. She had nothing against eryngium but they weren't anchusas and they were unstoppable. They tap-danced throughout her beds.

She perservered, however, purchasing three baby anchusas. Sadly the little plants hardly survived beyond four inches. And they were the first of many miscarried anchusas.

'Fifth time lucky!' choruses Maud-Next-Door as she watches the AG carefully surround the tiny anchusas with generously enriched compost before patting them tenderly yet firmly into place. Brushing soil from her hands, she sits back and smiles at her neighbour.

'Oh, I do hope so!' she exclaims.

'Be delighted by hope, not merely persecuted or protected by it,' quotes Maud, who has recently begun reading psychotherapist Adam Phillips.

The AG is haunted by the quotation. Be delighted by hope she tells herself as she nurtures the new arrivals. She waters them at the first inkling of drought, she provides them with nourishing foliar feeds and chases away anything that impinges on their light and space. She is allowing herself to anticipate the pleasures of adult anchusas when disaster strikes. An anchusa vanishes. Sadly she inspects the wreckage left in the wake of a marauding predator. But determined that hope shall be not persecuting but protective, she settles bright green plastic slug and snail-proof rings around the remaining plants.

The AG has yet to encounter a plant that's averse to snail collars. Being swaddled in green plastic seems to provoke growth and they soon protrude safely above their protective collars. Not so the anchusas. Hating captivity, slowly they wilt, droop and die.

'It's so unfair!' the AG cries aloud. 'It's hopeless!'

Maud-Next-Door, reading on her patio, looks up from Adam Phillips, 'Rage is the last vestige of hope!' she quotes.

The anxious gardener
pursues the perfect rose

She knows it's a cliché, but nevertheless the Anxious Gardener longs for the perfect red rose. It must be disease resistant, almost continually in flower with nicely packed petals and plentiful glossy foliage. It must look on the wild side; nothing like a hybrid tea. It must have an old-fashioned air yet bear no resemblance to those modern 'old-fashioned' roses with their globular heads and packed petals. Somewhere she knows her dream rose is waiting for her. She pours over Peter Beale's catalogue and Austin's roses as others might surf the net in search of the perfect partner.

Then, on her own doorstep, the dream rose materialises. Taking out the rubbish, she glances at the house two doors down. Unbelievably, abseiling up the front elevation is a potential candidate: a rich dark red, the right size, well-clothed with leaves and loaded with optimistic buds.

She compares the Right Rose with 'Souvenir du Docteur Jamain' lurking glumly beside her own front door. Dr Jamain, clotted with aphids, is playing host to a viticella clematis which is fast suffocating the rose. Pessimistic about Dr Jamain's flowering possibilities, the AG had planted 'Polish Spirit' to conceal the rose's failings and now the poor rose was bowed down by the weight of the flourishing clematis.

The AG sighs. Silently she endows the growers of the Right Rose with all the gardening gifts she suddenly feels she lacks. She just knows that they are energetic, efficient and endowed with an inexhaustible supply of horticultural inside knowledge. Envy has her in its grip.

'I do know how you feel,' says Maud-Next-Door, materializing at her side and taking in the difference between the

'All relationships require a degree of compromise,' replies
the Anxious Gardener, gazing fondly at 'Blush Noisette'

Right Rose and 'Souvenir du Docteur Jamain'. 'It reminds me of how I felt when Selma at number 38 got into that school . . . what's it called? It begins with H. Clarice, of course, fell at the first post. Why don't you ring their bell and ask the Name of the Rose?'

'I couldn't.'

'Don't be such a shrinking violet. I'll come and hold your hand.'

They pause at the gate. The AG gazes up at her ideal. 'Stop!' she cries, 'Look at that!' Close up, she sees that the dream rose is heavily powdered with mildew. The leaves are crinkling with mould. Envy evaporates at the sight. She retrieves all the horticultural abilities she had only just projected into the rose's owners; she is convinced they are the type of irresponsible gardeners who underfeed and allow the roots of roses to dry out. As for the Right Rose, it's clearly the Wrong Rose.

'Will I ever find the perfect red climber?' she asks the Gardening Mentor.

'Let me see. What about 'Soldier Boy' or 'Dortmund'? They are both wonderfully disease-resistant and flower all season.'

'Sorry, they're single roses. No, it's not that I'm a slave to fashion. It's that single roses bloom for such a short time.'

'OK, how about the semi-double, reasonably small-flowered 'Parkdirektor Riggers'?'

'I know the catalogues advertise him as disease-free but in my experience he comes down with mildew every year.'

'Personally, I don't think you can beat 'Guinée'. Such a wonderful deep, dark, velvet red. But knowing the guilt induced in you by black spot and rust, growing 'Guinée' could just provoke the onset of depression.'

'Flowers too hefty, leaves too sick,' replies the AG.

'I know! The perfect rose for you is a rambler called 'Chevy Chase'. The flowers are small, multi-petaled and a wonderful red, and it never has a day's illness.'

'I don't want a rambler. They grow too tall.'

'Face it, with a wish list like yours you're condemned to do without red roses. Grit your teeth and settle for pink. They are so much healthier.'

The AG researches pink roses. An elitist at heart, she rejects 'New Dawn' as too common while 'Albertine' is a shade too dark and what's more only flowers once in summer.

'Lower your sights,' says her mother. ' Really, darling, you can't beat a nice Hybrid Tea. I've one with simply enormous yellow flowers called Ethel. I highly recommend it.'

The AG shivers with disgust and perseveres searching for the right pink. It's then that she discovers 'Blush Noisette'. She had never imagined falling for a pink rose but 'Blush Noisette' could almost be described as white. Its plentiful pale green leaves show no sign of illness. Its trusses of small flowers are not overcrowded and the flowers repeat with stunning generosity all summer. And though it's not technically a climber, it can be easily convinced to cover a wall while staying within easy reach of her secateurs. She can dead-head without a ladder.

'But it's pink!' cries Maud.

'All relationships require a degree of compromise,' sagely replies the Anxious Gardener, gazing fondly at 'Blush Noisette'.

The anxious gardener
dreads seeming dated

The Anxious Gardener prides herself on appearing up to date. The width of her trousers contracts and expands, her belts thicken and thin, her fringe comes and goes according to a visceral compulsion. Or so she thinks. She considers herself not so much a follower of fashion but more as someone intuitively in step with the trends. She discovers, for example, that if she develops a yen for brown linen trousers, she's bound to find them on the rails.

Not so with her garden. She has become a horticultural dinosaur. Her garden is passé, out-moded, shamefully dated. Roses are permitted to be old-fashioned, but a garden blind to design developments is nothing more than an embarrassment. Recently the AG turned resolutely against the reintroduction of stiletto heels but that was a health issue. Nothing justifies a garden stuck in the stone age. In the era of *Ground Force* her garden is planted not designed. Not only does her garden consist of nothing but flower beds, it even lacks inserts that could bring it up to date.

The time has come 'to make a contemporary statement', decides the AG. Aluminium planters spring to mind. They could provide contemporary punctuation marks. But she just knows that every time she looks at them, she'll hear a hollow ring and remember that aluminium is implicated in the aetiology of Altzheimers.

'For God's sake, you won't be cooking with them or drinking out of them!' exclaims the Gardening Mentor who has a penchant for aluminium planters. The AG decides to stick to terracotta.

Then there's decking. The problem is the AG feels on firmer ground with stone. Wood rots.

'You paint on preservative,' explains the GM.

Alliums are so this year

'It smells and it's bound to be carcinogenic,' answers the AG.

A water feature, she thinks, would really bring the garden into the twenty-first century. At the Chelsea Flower Show the AG had been very taken with a sheet of shining metal flowing with water. But would a continuously pouring metal sheet blend with a Victorian terraced house?

Then the AG remembers painted concrete and plaster. She could plaster the back wall and paint it white or blue and insert pieces of coloured glass. It would stylishly elongate the entire garden.

'Think of moss and lichen climbing the wall in the winter,' warns the GM. 'It would be simpler to just swop your garden furniture. Chuck out all that chunky old-fashioned wood and replace it with steel. Instant face-lift!'

The AG looks fondly at her table and chairs, so comfortable, so natural, and imagines spindly steel scraping on the stones of the patio.

'OK, how about a pergola?'

Briefly the AG brightens. She can imagine clematis, climbing roses and perhaps a honeysuckle, despite its tendency to bugs, snaking up a pergola. But her garden suffers from sun deprivation. How could it possibly accommodate the added shade of a pergola?

'Well, in that case it's down to your planting scheme. A couple of Italian topiary spirals would do the world for your garden. And of course you could add a phormium, a cordyline, a tree fern and a palm. These days you can buy a blue hesper palm for only seventy-five pounds. Amazing isn't it?'

Silently the AG calculates how many of her favourite perennials she could purchase for the cost of the palm. She thinks of dozens of different salvias, penstemons, a couple of new China roses and a *Trachelospermum jasminoides*.

'Then there are grasses,' continues the GM. 'They provide a really Now sense of sound and movement. Grasses are still really today.'

'They don't flower,' murmurs the AG.

'Of course, they do. Think of pearl grass with all those invisible hairs dangling with white pearls. What's more, they come in all different shades of green and you can even get a black grass – the name escapes me.'

The AG visualizes a black and green, sparsely planted garden, with maybe a couple of shaped box plants, and a bit of sculpture to draw the eye.

'I can't . . .' she begins, feeling less and less flexible, more and more set in her ways and unavailable to the creative excitement of the contemporary world.

'Look, stop fretting,' interrupts the GM. 'You're fashionably unfashionable. You've a "cottage garden". And look at those alliums. They are so this year. Alliums were everywhere at Chelsea.'

The Anxious Gardener looks at her mauve alliums, waving globularly, fashionably in the wind, and is comforted.

The anxious gardener
is allergic to yellow

With her garden, the Anxious Gardener inherited a yellow climbing rose called 'Laura Ford', a yellow shrub rose and an indestructible buttercup-yellow *Hypericum* 'Hidcote'. Like an inescapable genetic condition, all three bloom in her soil. She hates them.

'A friend of mine gave birth to a ginger and got used it. You'll soon learn to love them,' said Maud-Next-Door, relishing the discordant notes jarring the discreet orchestration of the AG's garden.

But colour out of place literally pains the AG. Each time she goes into the garden, the yellow jumps out and hits her in the solar plexus.

Each time she goes into the garden, the yellow jumps out and hits her

'That's the whole point of yellow,' sighs the Gardening Mentor. 'It gives dynamism to a border. It's a forward colour.'

But the AG finds she is forever apologising for the forward nature of yellow. Just as she is compelled to acknowledge and ask forgiveness for imperfect cooking, so she compulsively explains that the presence of the Yellow Three is entirely accidental. She is not responsible. They preceded her into the garden.

'You are being ridiculous,' says the GM. 'Yellow is the most natural, Soil Association-approved colour you can get in a garden, with the exception of green. Think winter jasmine, think daffodils.'

'They're different. They're nature's answer to SAD.'

'You've got me there.'

'Seasonal Affective Disorder. Daffs are nature's lightboxes. In fact, yellow is acceptable in spring, just out of place in summer.'

'I'm going to be entirely frank with you,' says the GM. 'St John's wort is yellow.'

'So?'

'So for an anxious, easily depressed gardener, yellow flowered plants are a must. Yellow alyssum, epimedium, coreopsis, euphorbia, rudbeckia, helium, they're indestructible.'

'Save me from them.'

'If you are going to garden you've got to harden. A good gardener knows when to save and when to sacrifice. Get a spade, dig up the yellows, if you feel that strongly.'

Gripped by guilt, the AG surveys Laura Ford, a patio climber hiking up the trellis in a neat, controlled way. She flowers constantly, never suffers a day's illness and is too short to desert her for the neighbour's garden. She fears that the God of the Garden will punish her for the murder of Laura Ford. She tells herself she should be grateful. She might have inherited the shamelessly yellow 'Lady Hillingdon' or 'Golden Showers'. Laura Ford, after an embarrassing moment, fades to an acceptable yellow. Who was Laura Ford? Most modern patio climbers have names like 'Nice Day' or 'Warm Welcome'. She can imagine killing off 'Nice Day' but not Laura Ford. Perhaps she could put her up for adoption. She phones all the gardeners she knows but no one is prepared to take the rose.

The hypericum bursts into flower in June, clashing with the nearby hydrangea, undermining the cerise rose 'Marjorie Fair' and extinguishing the small, delicate pink flowers of the 'Grootendorst' rose. In despair, the AG thinks that it's as if the Queen were planted in her border dressed in a heavy silk yellow coat with handbag, hat and high heels dyed to match. Filled with republican zeal she hurries to her mobile. She texts the Gardening Mentor: 'HRH gotta go. Plse cme armd w. spde.'

The anxious gardener ## *wants to be ecologically sound*

The Anxious Gardener gardens for pleasure and to please, yet she is forever incurring disapproval.

She tries her best to be ecologically sound; going cold turkey on insecticide, importing beneficial predators, eschewing endangered peat, and liberally feeding the birds. She is, nevertheless, always one step behind her critics and forever in the horticultural wrong.

Take the patio. Forced by cats using the lawn as a public convenience to evict the grass, she was enormously appreciative of her patio, which obviated sado-masochistic mowing. Of course, she had protected her mother from the loss of the lawn, knowing how loudly she'd mourn the passing of the grass. It hadn't been easy keeping the secret of the stone, as gardening news was guaranteed to satisfactorily fill empty

These thugs are seeing off the native bluebell

patches during phone calls. But she'd done it. What she hadn't anticipated was the shocked response of friends and fellow gardeners.

'You realise you're contributing to the risk of London flooding,' said Mary, eyeing the patio with deep distaste. The AG owned up to thoughtlessness. Flooding London was the last thing she had had in mind when the Gardening Mentor laid the patio for her.

'It's people like you, digging up grass and concreting front gardens, who prevent rain water sinking into soil as it naturally would.' The AG listened humbly and guiltily, but decided that though it constituted an ecological threat, her handsome patio, nicely fringed with ground-cover plants, would stay in place.

Then there was the Spanish bluebell problem. She adores her little patch of bluebells redolent of woodland and returning each spring to flower alongside daffodils, muscari and anemones.

'Oh my God!' exclaimed a visiting friend, an activist in the campaign to keep British flora and fauna British, 'You're choosing to grow Spanish bluebells!' The AG, previously ignorant of the country of origin of her bluebells, was loud in her defence of the immigrants.

'What you don't understand,' sighed her friend, 'is that these thugs are seeing off the native bluebell. Growing them is tantamount to shooting red squirrels.'

The AG hangs on to her bluebells but guilt gets the better of her where rue is concerned. Mary and her two children come to tea on a fine sunny day. While the women drank tea and ate carrot cake, the children watered the garden and each other.

The AG basked in a sense of plenitude until Mary screamed, jumped to her feet and pulled the children away from the garden.

'You're growing rue!' she gasped. 'How could you? Do

you have any idea of what it can do? Why do you think it's called rue?'

The AG admitted ruefully that she had no idea the plant caused serious skin lesions. She promised to evict the beautiful blue-green rue from her garden. The loss was, however, tempered by the satisfaction of being horticulturally correct – and her mild aversion to the plant's yellow flower.

The anxious gardener

takes against pinching out

The Anxious Gardener has never pinched out, but a late-June gardening column warns of dire consequences if she fails to attend to the growing tips of late-flowering perennials. Unless she excises the tips of her asters and rudbeckias they will grow tall, spare and insecure. Pinching out produces, solid, well-rounded citizens.

'If you stop them shooting upwards, then obviously they'll bush out,' the Gardening Mentor tells her.

But the words 'pinching out' worry the Anxious Gardener. They evoke the violent games of childhood. 'Pinch, punch, first of the month.' She wonders why the first of the month licensed aggression. 'Adam and Eve and Pinch Me went down to the sea to bathe. Adam and Eve were drowned, who do you think was saved?' She would cry, 'Pinch Me (not)' to no avail. Not only does pinching out suggest aggression but also theft. With one deft, vicious movement she will be stealing the heart of the plant.

Nevertheless, the AG goes and inspects her asters, grown for their late-flowering ability to ward off autumn leaf-fall depression. She has two sorts: the taller *Aster ericoides*, with each stem bearing crowds of small, airy flowers, and the dwarf *Aster dumosus*. She bends down to the

Unless she excises the tips of her asters, they will grow tall, spare and insecure. Pinching out produces solid citizens

latter which has grown into a thick satisfying mat, full of promise. Surely it is sufficiently low and bushy not to need to be stopped in its tracks. Tentatively she picks the heart from one stem and pulls apart the cone of tightly curled, pale green leaves. Anxiously she searches for a foetal flower.

'Isn't there a risk that pinching out will pinch an embryonic flower?' she asks the GM.

'It would be a very premature baby. The flowers are not due till late July or August or even later. We're only in June.'

Still the AG feels uneasy in relation to the procedure.

'It doesn't feel natural. It's like docking a poodle's tail or stapling the tips of a Shetland sheepdog's ear.'

The GM sighs audibly.

'When you dock a tail, does it encourage the growth of side tails? No it doesn't. Whereas when you pinch out growing tips it encourages lateral flower growth. You hate staking. I offer you a means of circumventing it and you start worrying about poodle's ears.'

'Collie's ears!'

But the AG does hate staking, either she throttles a plant or fails to provide adequate support. So she sets about removing the tips of her asters under the watchful eye of Maud-Next-Door who peers through the trellis. The AG explains, a shade defensively, that it may look like mass destruction but in fact she is paving the way for lateral growth and numerous flowers.

'I see!' cries Maud. 'It's like pulling out grey hairs. Three grow back for every one plucked out.'

The anxious gardener
insists on monogamy

Ignoring cries of moral outrage and declarations of hatred, the Anxious Gardener taught her children to share their toys. And she shared her children. She spread them round godmothers, stepmothers, grandmothers and other mothers, without a qualm. But she can't share her garden. She is a fiercely possessive, monogamous, single-handed gardener. She has been known to employ professionals for back-breaking tasks, for as she says, she has never felt jealous of a lover's dentist or doctor. But just the thought of division of labour in the garden makes her anxious.

She listens with disbelief when gardeners of her acquaintance extol the advantages of shared gardening. Usually they practise a conventional gender division of labour, he mows and she weeds, he digs and she dead-heads. The AG knows that in comparable circumstances, as soon as she abandoned mowing the lawn to a partner, she would disown the grass – simply cease to see it.

She is forced to confront her horticultural monogamy when a visiting gardener offers to do a little dead-heading.

'It's fine, really, honestly, don't feel you have to,' stutters the AG.

Ignoring her protestations, delighted to be gainfully employed, the visitor seizes the secateurs and advances on 'Little White Pet', a short, small-flowered rose, almost continually in flower and hence in need of a good dead-head. The AG itches to rip the secateurs from her friend's fingers as chunks of 'Little White Pet' hit the earth.

'An awful lot of nonsense is talked about rose pruning,' declares the friend as she hacks at the rose. 'There is absolutely no need to make a slanting cut against an outward facing bud. They did a study of roses that just had the

Come summer the bright pink lilies shot up and
shot to pieces her carefully planned colour scheme

shears taken to them and those that were pruned according to the rules. Guess which group did best?'

The AG surveys the remains of 'Little White Pet'. She has no desire to go to its aid. Silently she repudiates the rose. It's as if her relationship with the plant had been dead-headed.

'Was she right?' she asks the Gardening Mentor over the phone. 'Is it OK to randomly chop a rose?'

'Not according to my books it isn't. A slanting cut stops water gathering on the incision, which in turn stops rot, while a neat cut against a bud gives shape and purpose. You don't want a lot of dead end twiggy bits, do you? On the other hand, there is a school of thought that says just leave the plant well alone, it needs as much foliage as possible to catch the sun.'

The AG hangs up. Normally, contradictory advice on rose care would raise her blood pressure, but her mind is on horticultural monogamy. She lets others cut her hair, she has successfully co-authored books, she has no problems letting others feed the cats, but the idea of another foot on the spade is anathema. It's akin to sexual jealousy, she decides. She remembers her mother telling her that one act of infidelity leaves a third body forever in the bed. It's the same with a flower bed she decides, recalling the pink lily incident.

It would be too strong a word to say she had felt ravaged by the incident but she had certainly felt violated. A well-meaning cat-sitter had slipped some lily bulbs into her beds. Come summer the bright pink lilies shot up and shot to pieces her carefully planned colour scheme. It had taken her months to regain a relationship of trust and intimacy with her borders.

The anxious gardener
takes up arms against a sea of climbers

The Anxious Gardener is faced with a crowd of uninvited visitors. There's a Russian vine arriving from the east, a *Clematis montana* from the west, ivy from the north and a *Jasminum officinale* from the south. She's nothing against any of them personally, except perhaps the Russian vine, whose task is defined as clothing the unsightly, and she resents the implication that her garden falls into that category. But the fact remains that they are other people's children.

Each summer she smartly snips the Russian vine back to where it belongs, saving her hydrangea and her Hybrid Musk rose, 'Felicity', from its unwanted embrace. Yet she feels as furtive as if she were, indeed, cutting the hair of another woman's child.

'More like slapping someone else's unruly kid,' says the Gardening Mentor. 'No one in their right mind grows a Russian vine. Not for nothing is it known as mile-a-minute.'

But then there are the welcome guests; the line of grape vine, the loop of white clematis. Encouraging them seems like seducing a neighbouring cat. 'Do you think it's stealing?' she asks as she snips a bunch of dark purple grapes.

'Think of it as giving a good home to a stray.'

'I'd like to think I'd take in a rescue cat, but give me a cat in kittenhood and I'll show you a cat whose habits match my own.'

'No comment.'

Of course, plants have set off from her garden to flourish in her neighbour's. It reminds her of when her son left home. She suffered awful anxiety about his diet, envisaging an exclusive intake of chips and pizza. She is convinced that next door doesn't foliar-feed 'Parkdirektor Riggers' – a

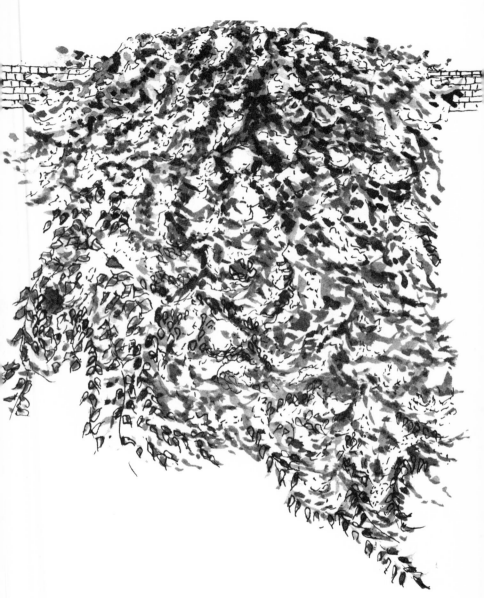

'You can't bear distance (the Russian vine is planted on my side) and you can't bear closeness (it's coming over to your side).'

promiscuous red climber that divides itself between her own and her neighbour's trellis.

Unbeknownst to the AG she has been observed ridding her garden of the Russian vine. It's owner, Maud-Next-Door, is not best pleased.

'What are you doing to my vine?'

'The question surely should be what is it doing to my rose and to my hydrangea,' snaps the AG, caught in the act, secateurs gaping.

'I'm in my rights, you know.'

'You are in your rights legally, but psychologically just how right-minded are you?' Maud retorts, heavily identified with her unwanted climber. 'You have a real problem with intimacy. You can't bear distance (it's planted on my side) and you can't bear closeness (it's coming over to your side).'

The AG is incensed. Surely a little light pruning shouldn't provoke wild analysis. 'I'm not averse to intimacy but I won't stand by and see my hydrangea groped,' she answers trying, and failing dismally, to sound a light note.

'Now, now, ladies!'

As one the Anxious Gardener and Maud turn on the Gardening Mentor. Neighbourly relations are saved, as together they chorus 'We're not ladies and we're most certainly not lady gardeners!'

The anxious gardener
accepts ageing unwillingly

The Anxious Gardener is wedded to the idea of progress. Believing everything she reads on labels and in gardening manuals, she eagerly anticipates each plant's future development. Impatiently she awaits the moment when the promised clump forms, the wands stretch skywards, the anticipated

Nipping and tucking, lifting and dividing never
retrieve the first flush of flowery youth

height arrives and the spread spreads.

But she hasn't bargained on the brevity of perfection. She feeds, waters and watches for the clump to form and the flowers to flush, only to discover that after a brief flawless moment, it's downhill all the way. The perfect clump proceeds to fragment, to crowd its neighbours, to hurl itself from the bed and to grow too tall for its own good.

'How often do I have to tell you? The solution is to cut back, lift and divide and provide support,' says the Gardening Mentor when the AG laments the limp, bowed and bent spires of vebascum which had reached for the sky for all of one day.

But the AG knows that, like plastic surgery, the GM's answer to slumped stems is fundamentally no answer. Nipping and tucking, lifting and dividing and supporting never retrieve the first flush of flowery youth. Indeed, the vebascum standing stock still against its bamboo evokes a botoxed forehead.

It's not only individual plants that pass their prime at top speed, it's that planting triumphs are evanescent. Successful plant associations are temporary affairs. Her garden is littered with memories of great moments in her gardening history. She recalls the time when the clematis 'Niobe' and the climbing rose 'Guinée' achieved simultaneous orgasm. Despite her best efforts they had never mingled again in quite the same way. 'Guinée' had climbed out of reach of 'Niobe', which had tangled amongst the lower reaches of the rose. Then there had been the combination of the rose 'Velchenbrau' – a dark, mauve-pink – with the mallow 'Barnsley' and a purple buddleia. 'Barnsley' died young; 'Velchenbrau' developed a seemingly incurable disease. Only the buddleia soldiered on in solitary splendour.

One day in late May, the AG celebrates an almost perfect border moment with a combination of four plants of exactly the same age – in their prime. A pale blue *Iris reticulata* stands in a generous, thick, perfectly circular clump behind a well-formed purple salvia, while pink-mauve sweet rocket snakes between the two, and a maroon aquilegia waves near by.

'They'll be over soon,' said Maud-Next-Door. 'You should snap them.'

'Snap them?'

'Yes and arrange the snaps in an album. I did that with the children just before they broke out. I knew it was coming. Acne runs and runs in the family. So I got some gorgeous snaps while they were still clear. I knew they would never be the same again.'

But the AG finds photos no solution. They induce nostalgia and dissatisfaction with the present. She knows she must struggle to value the natural; crowsfeet and bent verbascum, double chins and splayed violas.

The anxious gardener
dislikes July

Fruitful summer ends with the last set at Wimbledon; all that's left is drought and uncomfortably hot holidays, thinks the Anxious Gardener as she turns off the television and turns towards the garden. Depression cloaks her, rendering her as tired as her plants.

Time, high winds and heavy summer rain have played havoc with everything in the garden. Even recent arrivals like the viticella clematis are looking distinctly battered, losing their grip on the trellis and bringing roses down with them onto the patio. The broad leaves of the *Salvia uliginosa* have hit the ground and stayed there. The rose 'New Dawn' has given up the effort to flower and the buds have balled and rotted. The climbing rose 'Parkdirektor Riggers', despite water-

Dead-heading is just a last ditch stand against death

ing, feeding and illicit spraying has yet again succumbed to mildew. The mallow has hung its head and hidden its flowers. Like roasted vegetables, plants are browning at the edges; shrivelled bits of foliage everywhere catch the AG's weary eye. The AG is a poor nurse to the elderly. The possibility of progress is the stuff of life to her. The prospect of the irreversible decline of the garden sends her back to the television. She switches on highlights from Wimbledon.

'Abuse of the elderly is as widespread as abuse of children,' says the Gardening Mentor reprovingly, finding her slumped in front of the set. 'Your garden needs you. Get out there and dead-head.'

Even the words 'dead-head' discourage the Anxious Gardener. Weeding, feeding, staking, are all about growth. Dead-heading is just a last ditch stand against death. Nevertheless, she goes in search of the secateurs, locating them just as her mobile phone vibrates with a message. She fishes it from her jeans pocket. The GM is never one to let a subject drop. 'To counter that late summer sense of deprivation, to fill that sense of emptiness I proscribe a mix of: fuchsia, *Ceratostigma willmotianum*, lilies, penstemon, dahlias (but mind the slugs), *Nerine bowdenii, Geranium* 'Ann Folkard' and hydrangea.'

'Anti-depressants dull the pain/obscure the problem,' she replies but in fact she has already planted late flowerers in anticipation of July-gloom. However, late flowerers are solitary voices rather than the orchestral arrangement of plants she loves in June.

Nevertheless, once in the garden, gloom lifts. The sun shines, birds sing and cats relax on the patio. She begins to envisage a future, as shrivelled rose blooms fall beneath her secateurs, and in her imagination, new buds spring from her neat slanting cuts.

'Dead-heading?' asks Maud-Next-Door, observing her through the trellis.

'What does it look like?' the AG longs to reply and in her irritation, snips not spent flowers but new buds from the rose 'Clair Matin'.

'You know what repeat roses bring to mind,' says Maud undeterred, 'sex in long-term relationships.'

'Why?' asks the AG unable to help herself.

'Nothing ever compares to the first flush,' answers Maud.

'Oh, but that's not true. Hybrid Musks get better and better, producing sumptuous autumn flowers.'

'They do, do they?' says Maud significantly.

Flustered and ever more irritated, the AG once more inadvertently dead-heads a bit of rose with future potential. Silently she apologises to the bush she has vandalised.

'I have to say,' says Maud, sensing hostility and fighting back, 'Your garden looks a touch mid-life.'

'Meaning?'

'Well, the harsh thing about the forties,' replies Maud, 'is that there's still the possibility of achievement but the prospects are slim. Same with your garden, it's still looking good but it's evident that its future prospects are poor.'

The AG springs to the defence of her plants, pointing out the hydrangea poised on the point of flowering, the lily buds full of promise and the flowers gracing the fuchsia wands. Maud, however, continues to mull over the meanings of the decades.

'Personally, I prefer the fifties. Oppressive expectations disappear and it becomes perfectly acceptable to spend Saturday night at home. Such a relief. I love to see a tidy, well-cut-back autumnal garden.'

'I suppose you're hinting that my garden could do with some blue-rinse conifers, some evergreens for year-round structure.'

'Well, I wasn't but now you mention it, I think you could do with some mahonias. They really do lighten the dark days of winter with their yellow flowers.'

The AG conjours up a picture of a mahonia, one plant she particularly dislikes. She visualizes their harsh stems, their prickly, leathery leaves; aggressive, and unchanging. Is that what she wants? An evergreen, monotonous garden to greet the end of Wimbledon? Affectionately she surveys her tousled, windswept plot, in the throes of its mid-life crisis.

The anxious gardener *has a moment of optimism*

Like an unplanned but welcome pregnancy, the Anxious Gardener's August garden flowers unexpectedly. Dwarf dahlias that she had left neglected in the ground last year appear and survive the slugs to provide powerful red and white punctuation marks across the flower beds. Polemium that had long been and gone in spring, throw up new spikes of mauve flowers amongst pale pink obedience plants. The tall, thin, mauve and pink wands wave in unison. Meanwhile, on the wall behind them, a dark purple clematis, 'Polish Spirit', flowers apologetically late, long after the AG had given it up for lost to clematis wilt. Perhaps most startling was the sudden appearance of a tropaeolum which she had planted almost ten years ago and despaired of. She had positioned it where it could scramble over a tall box shrub. She had anticipated the small, dark green leaves of the box, enlivened by the scarlet climbing tropaeolum. In vain had she waited for the tropaeolum to start scaling the shrub. Disconsolately it lurked at the foot of the box before disappearing altogether. It is clearly a plant with a mind of its own because when it mysteriously reappears it ignores the box in favour of a 'Clair Matin' rose. The pink rose sits a little uneasily with the scarlet tropaeolum but the AG is utterly delighted. She had forgotten the climber had ever existed.

Like an unplanned but welcome pregnancy
the August garden flowers unexpectedly

'It's nothing short of supernatural,' she exclaims to the Gardening Mentor. 'I am blessed amongst gardeners.'

'It's less a case of supernatural intervention than timely use of shears and secateurs. You did as I told you. You swallowed your sentimentality and cut back in time, not sparing even a stem. Those valerian flowering over there, the campanulas and the scabious have all risen again in defiance of your dead-heading. Congratulations!'

The AG modestly casts her eyes down to the York stone at her feet. She feels fruitful. You have to be cruel to be kind, she thinks. Getting the children to bed early, slimming the cat, shearing the aubretias – all painful at the time but rewarding in the long run. Yet there *were* happy accidents. She had had a hand in neither the return of the dahlias nor the resurrection of the 'Polish Spirit' viticella clematis. And she had certainly done nothing at all to earn the reappearance of the tropaeolum, ten years after its apparent demise. Horticultural surprise gifts are balm to the soul of a pessimistic plantswoman.

The anxious gardener
fails to leave well alone

'There comes a point in the gardening year when you just have to lay off. And we've reached it. There is nothing you can do. There is nothing you should do,' decrees the Gardening Mentor.

'Negative capability,' murmurs the Anxious Gardener.

'Not negative, just realistic,' replies the GM. 'September is upon us and the rain has done its worst and flattened all before it. Apparently it was the wettest August on record. You have to learn to be zen in the face of the weather.'

The AG looks round the garden and despondency swamps

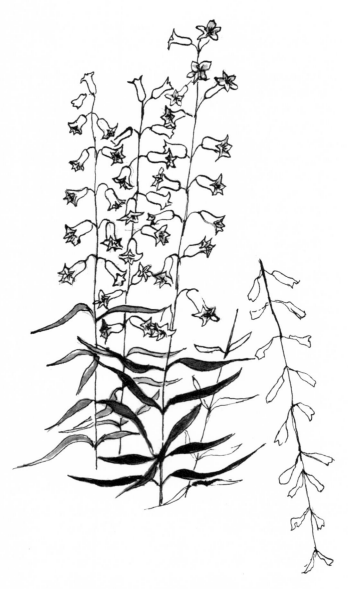

A leggy penstemon bites the dust before it has a chance to flower

her. Even late-flowering plants like eupatorium, which can be relied to remain on their feet and upright in all circumstances, have fallen forward, noses to the ground. Geraniums, habitually modest in the spatial requirements, having grown lush in the wet weather, occupy new tracts of territory. Other plants have way exceeded their normal height and plunged to earth. Meanwhile, opportunistic weeds, thriving in the damp, moist soil, have colonised previously weed-free spaces. A stinging nettle has risen in the centre of a clump of asters. The last straw, thinks, the AG pulling on her gloves.

'Stop,' cries the GM. 'Half the aster will come up with the nettle. Just ignore it!'

How can the AG ignore creeping chaos? She lives in a world of hair straighteners, orthodontics, air-brushed photographs and cosmetic surgery.

Horticultural disorder and asymmetry are unbearable. A white monarda has crashed down on top of a sedum that has yet to flower, an obedience plant is bearing down on the monarda. A wandering eryngium has penetrated and towers above a low-growing cistus. An abnormally thick clump of polemonium thrives in the front of the border, obscuring all behind it.

'Just let it all die down. Right now you can't see the wood for the trees.'

'Flowers from the weeds.'

'Whatever, but I'm warning you. Some of the greatest horticultural errors have been committed out of shame and impatience.'

But the Anxious Gardener can't help herself. As soon as the coast is clear she seizes a hand fork and secateurs. Hungry for order she advances on the tangled beds. Sacrificing both the dead and the living, ruthlessly she snips and uproots. A leggy penstemon bites the dust before it has a chance to flower. A *Knautia macedonica* still in full flower is decapitated to stop it sprawling. A foxglove is sacrificed for the sake of neatness. The AG ploughs through the bed, unstoppable in her zeal. Then disaster strikes. Around the feet of the rose 'Clair Matin' is a luxurious, trespassing growth of grass. Furiously the AG seizes it, tugs at it and in her enthusiasm severs the growing stem of a tropaeolum lurking unseen amongst the grass.

'Oh, I'm so, so sorry,' she cries as the plant's scarlet flowers droop and prepare to die. Hot, bothered and contrite, the AG leaves the scene of the crime.

The anxious gardener

encounters envy

The Anxious Gardener can sense the gritted teeth of denied envy behind the request 'We'd love to see the garden.' More destructive than aphids, hungrier than caterpillars, more smothering than snails in its ravages, the AG dreads envy. Conducting her visitors towards the garden, in her mind, she marshals defensive denigration of her beloved plot. She wonders how people who open their gardens to the public deflect envy.

Sometimes the envious attack is masked as solidarity: 'I see you too have problems pruning wisteria.' Then there's the sympathetic smile and the crooked eyebrow while the AG gazes at the wisteria, which, in a matter of moments, changes from luxuriant and rampant to horribly tangled.

Confession concealing denigration is a common ploy of the envious gardener, 'Oh, I wish I had time to make something like this of my garden. Aren't you lucky!' The AG is left feeling at once overprivileged and underemployed – an unfairly advantaged, yet essentially marginal, figure with too much time on her hands. 'It must bring you a lot of pleasure,'

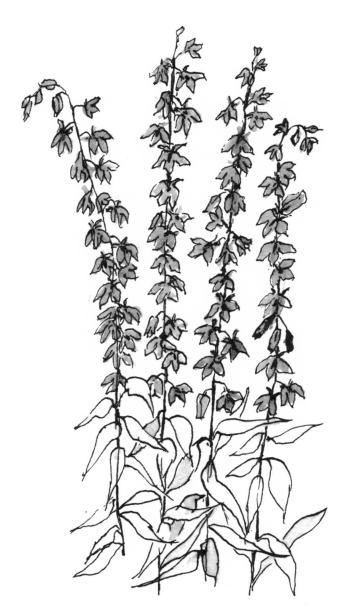

Lobelia envy is virulent

continues the visitor, while the AG wracks her brain for defensive evidence of pain and examples of frustration.

'You're paranoid,' the Gardening Mentor tells her.

'I'm not. It's just an impossible situation. Part of the pleasure of gardening is Show and Tell, which inevitably evokes envy. Take the case of that lobelia over there, that incredible magenta lobelia. I was so excited by that lobelia. I hauled my friend Mary into the garden to see it. She looked at it and murmured, 'Do you know, I've never had a lobelia come up the following year. Maybe you'll have better luck.'

'So it was good of her to wish you luck with the lobelia.'

'You don't hear the subtext? She wants my lobelia to disappear without trace. She couldn't bear for mine to flourish when hers has died. Lobelia-rivalry is virulent.'

Sometimes envy prompts actual destruction with ground cover ground beneath a boot, a football aimed accidentally at the heart of a kolkowitzia, a flower plucked without permission. 'Sorry, I couldn't resist.'

Then there's the faux faux pas. 'That rose looks just as wonderful dead as alive, doesn't it,' exclaims an acquaintance. 'Actually,' answers the AG, 'it's not dead; it simply hangs its head as China roses are wont to do.' But the unconsciously desired damage is done.

The anxious gardener
gets depressed

The onset of her depression coincides with the first autumn gardening columns.

'If you want to get next year off to a bright start, now's the time to plant some eye-catching bulbs. John Negus springs into action . . .' The Anxious Gardener plunges into depression. It's all so pointless. She sees herself obediently hurrying

to the garden centre, pressing daffodils to check their firmness, scrutinizing tulips for mildew, struggling to purchase
varieties that will obediently flower in quick succession. And
for what? For bitter disappointments: bulbs that throw up
foliage devoid of flowers, leaves that flop, bulbs that become
squirrel fodder, bulbs that gently rot out of sight. Bulbs are
easy; bulbs are cheap, she tells herself. But that simply raises
the psychic failure stakes. She has only herself to blame when
things go wrong.

Gardening columns, waxing lyrical and littered with
encouraging language, simply serve to deepen her sense of
discouragement. 'Sporting sulphur-yellow trumpet blooms
amid a rosette of shining, bronzy-mottled leaves,
Erythronium 'Pagoda' is a dog's-tooth violet that lights up
April and May. Happiest in dappled-shade, in damp, humus-
rich soil, it looks great paired with miniature hostas.'

'Ha!' exclaims the AG. 'How long would a miniature
hosta last in my garden? The time it took for a miniature
snail to cross the path.'

'It's perfectly true that as a gardener you're dealing with
death but there's also annual resurrection,' says the
Gardening Mentor.

'Not so much death as murder,' replies the AG from the
depths of depression. 'Not so much resurrection as lucky
escape.'

'She continues to scan the gardening column: 'Nestle
Sanguinare canadensis among a patch of blush purple, ivy-
leaved *Hepatica nobilis* and create a real talking point.' I'd
settle for contemptuous silence, thinks the AG.

'You're suffering from leaf-fall depression,' says the GM
wanting to be kind. 'Come November you'll be out planting
your species tulips with the rest of us.'

'Don't patronise her,' shouts the AG's daughter from her
deckchair on the patio. 'She's seen the light! Finally she realises
that gardening is fundamentally boring, repetitive and

depressing. And what's more it's big business. All those new varieties, longer flowering seasons, double this and dwarf that are simply the flowering of capitalism.' She smiles, pleased with 'the flowering of capitalism'.

'Capitalism or optimism?' murmurs the GM.

'Capitalism,' snarls the daughter. 'Take a look at that.' She lobs a garden catalogue.

Listlessly the AG turns the pages of the bulb catalogue. It's the words that catch her eye: 'new', 'improved', 'robust'. There's a new, improved form of *Allium moly*. A new, improved snowflake with many large pure white bells with each segment tipped greenish yellow. 'Very robust.' The new, improved striped squill, 'very bright China-blue with a touch of ultramarine', sounds utterly delightful and 'is a remarkable improvement on the common form. The plants are more robust and the flowers much larger.' Then there's a new mauve and white tulip. The growers declare themselves 'proud to introduce this fantastic new variety'.

Slowly a sense of purpose grows; a hunger for possession energises, hope returns. The new improved versions are surely hardy enough to withstand even the Anxious Gardener.

'It's perfectly true that as a gardener you're dealing with death, but there's also annual resurrection,' says the Gardening Mentor

ACKNOWLEDGMENTS

I am most grateful to Dylan Singh for providing the professional answers, to Jean Sturgis for the drawings, which so sensitively interpret the text, to my editor Jo Christian and to my agent Veronique Baxter. Special thanks are due to the late Brenny Dunkley, Brian Foster, Ruthie Petrie, Jennifer Silverstone, Alison Swan Parente, to my family and above all to my mother, who was a passionate and assertive gardener.